Geoffrey Smith's World of Flowers

Part Two

BRITISH BROADCASTING CORPORATION

Geoffrey Smith's World of Flowers

Part Two

Edited by Brian Davies

Introduction

Plants, fortunately, pay no heed to international boundaries. *Lilium pardalinum*, the leopard lily, growing wild in the giant redwood forests on the Californian coast, will accept, without obvious discomfort, being transplanted to a woodland in England. *Pelargonium peltatum*, the ivy-leaved geranium, growing on a South African hillside, may be seen covering a 12 feet high bush in thousands of flowers. It is our good fortune that the long trailing stems of *Pelargonium peltatum*, weaving themselves up through the thorn bush on that wild sun-baked hillside, flower with the same freedom when cascading down from a window box in Wapping.

Some of the plants in this book and in the second series of programmes made for BBC television were introduced into Britain centuries ago; others are comparative newcomers. All, without exception, carry with them a thread of human history. Plant hunters, explorers, traders, pioneers, wealthy amateur botanists on sight-seeing expeditions, and indeed people from almost every walk of life assisted in the discovery and introduction of so many of the well-loved plants which grace gardens in Britain today. The countries of the world supplied the material; human curiosity and courage provided the means; while gardeners subscribe the accolade of appreciation.

I am most indebted to Peter Barnes and Sabina Knees for checking the manuscript, thus helping me to avoid the major pitfalls of plant nomenclature.

My thanks also to Frank Holland whose application and patience throughout on the design of the book make even the most avid gardener seem impetuous by comparison.

To Mel Davies, whose superb pictures make each page a garden, I would just say 'Every one a Rembrandt – very well done'.

Finally, my grateful thanks to all the people who allowed us access to their gardens to photograph the flowers.

Contents

Above:
Geoffrey Smith at the home of *Lilium* 'Enchantment' in Oregon

Title page:
Narcissus pseudonarcissus happily naturalised in a woodland setting at the Savill gardens

Half title:
Fuchsia 'Snowcap'

All the colour photographs were specially taken for the BBC by Mel Davies

Published to accompany the second BBC television series *Geoffrey Smith's World of Flowers*
First broadcast on BBC2 early in 1984

Produced by Brian Davies

The programmes were prepared in consultation with the BBC Continuing Education Council

First published 1984

Published by the British Broadcasting Corporation, 35 Marylebone High Street, London W1M 4AA

Printed and bound in Wales by Severn Valley Press Ltd, Caerphilly, Mid-Glamorgan

Colour separation by Chelmer Litho Reproductions

Photoset in 10/12pt 'Monophoto' Plantin Light by Ace Filmsetting Ltd, Frome, Somerset

ISBN 0 563 21022 2

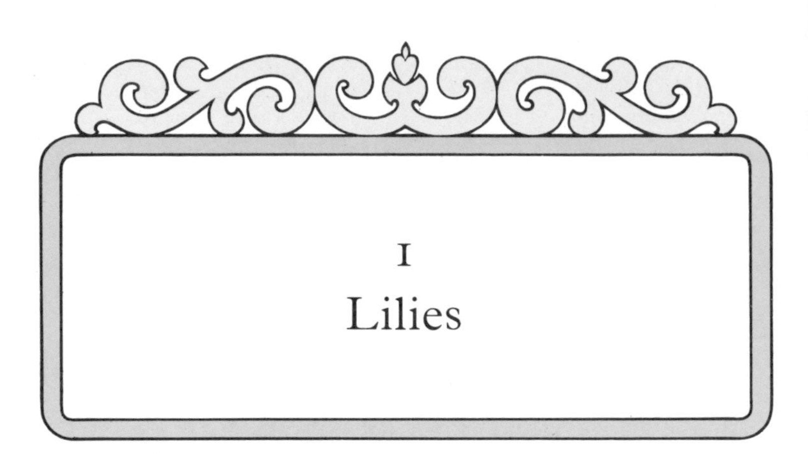

I
Lilies

The origins of so many garden plants are rooted in the mists of ancient civilisations. When and for what reason they were first cultivated is largely a matter of conjecture.

In the first century A.D., Pliny the Elder wrote in his *Natural History* that next to the rose there is no fairer flower or one of greater estimation than the lily. Pliny was, in fact, writing of a flower whose beauty had been appreciated for 2,500 years before he was born. Down through man's history the lily story can be traced. A fragment from a Cretan vase carries a lily flower motif. Assyrian architecture appreciates and records their beauty in stone. Greek and Roman writers extol the white flowers as an emblem of purity. *Lilium candidum*, the Madonna lily was, to early medieval writers and theologians, the celestial flower-emblem of St John the Baptist.

Lily bulbs made into a bread have been eaten by those suffering from dropsy, and the flowers infused in oil were applied to tumours. The petals when steeped in brandy were reputed to have powerful healing properties, and infusions of bulbs or petals were also prescribed in the treatment of coughs and asthma. Important though all these qualities must have been when medicine relied greatly on faith and little on science, it is as a garden flower that the lily has held a secure place over many centuries.

Precisely how many species of *Lilium* there are in cultivation is difficult to discover. A loose estimate of those native to temperate regions in the Northern Hemisphere would be between eighty and a hundred. Lilies are amongst the most beautiful of bulbous plants, though, as would be expected in so large a family with a wide diversity of habitats, not all of them are easily grown under garden conditions.

Most of the species grow in climates where the seasons are well defined – cold winters, a steady progression through spring to a dry summer with very hot sunshine. The bulbs are safe in winter under a covering of snow, then, during summer's drought, they are insulated by a mulch of rotting plant debris, their roots in many cases fed by moisture which percolates through the soil from melting snow. Indeed, when comparing the climate in this country with that enjoyed by lilies in their

Lilium candidum, the Madonna lily, in northern Greece

Asiatic and oriental hybrid lilies in a summer garden in Oregon

native habitat, it is surprising that so many of them survive and flourish.

In my experience, shelter is absolutely essential; lilies, more than most plants, detest being teased about by the wind or desiccated by draughts. A free-draining, lime-free soil which never dries out even in the hottest summer provides exactly the right root conditions. This is a situation I struggled to achieve on a heavy clay soil without success. Eventually, by raising the general level some 12 inches (30 cm) above that of the surrounding soil I provided conditions in which I grew over forty species and varieties very well. Given good drainage, most soils which are lime-free when prepared with generous dressings of humus in the form of rotted manure, peat, leaf mould, shredded bark or similar rottable material will grow lilies of quality. The ideal would be if the site sloped gently south west. A deep bed

Right: *Lilium bulbiferum croceum*

of humus topped up with 12 inches (30 cm) of sandy loam would grow any but the greenhouse lilies.

In areas where the soil is alkaline, the choice should be restricted to those species which are tolerant of lime and, indeed, there are a good number of these including such established favourites as *L. candidum*, *L. regale*, *L. martagon*, and *L. monadelphum*. *L. candidum*, the Madonna lily, is one of the oldest in cultivation, being featured on vases dating from the Minoan period. Where the Madonna lily originally came from is not certain, but it seems to be so well established in the Balkan Peninsula that this could be the natural home of this lovely lily. Hundreds of years before the birth of Christ it was being cultivated as a medicinal plant. No doubt, traders distributed bulbs throughout the Mediterranean region and, wherever it found conditions congenial, colonies grew. Thus it is now found as a garden escape in several regions of the Mediterranean. The conquering armies of Rome carried the bulbs to the furthest outposts of a vast empire once policed by the legions – possibly even to Great Britain where the Venerable Bede in his writings used it as a symbol of the Resurrection.

The monks of the Middle Ages cultivated *L. candidum* in their physic gardens alongside other medicinal plants. It is one of the hardiest, most easily cultivated of lilies, given conditions to suit it, though it is one of the species which defies exact definitions of cultivation. All that the optimistic gardener can do is plant the bulbs in late August into a lime soil – not too deeply, no more than 2 inches (5 cm) of loose soil above them. Within a few weeks basal leaves grow from scales in the centre of the bulb and, once established, it should be left undisturbed. Low-growing shrubs can be planted to supply root shade while still permitting the flowers to reach up to the sunlight. Only certain forms of the Madonna lily have ever seeded in my garden, and then only sparsely, in spite of my hand-pollination when the flowers appeared in early summer.

Lilium bulbiferum croceum, the orange lily, is a native of Savoy, Corsica, and Lombardy, and is a robust, easily grown bulb. The only difference that I can discover between this variety and *L. bulbiferum* is that of colour. The former has orange-petalled flowers, while those of *L. bulbiferum* have a distinct yellow overtone to the orange. Both will thrive in any ordinary garden soil, whether acid or alkaline, providing that the drainage is good. For centuries the orange lily has enjoyed the sort of popularity that only a tolerant, easily grown plant achieves. When left alone, it will in time form strong, well-flowered colonies. Both *L. bulbiferum croceum* and *L. bulbiferum*, unlike *L. candidum* which roots from the base of the bulb only, produce roots on the stem. This dual system of rooting is why so much importance is attached to making certain all lily bulbs are planted at the proper depth. The species that root from the base of the bulb only should be shallowly planted. Those that root from the base and from that part of the stem immediately above the bulbs need to be planted deeper – 5 inches (12.5 cm) or more instead of the 2 inches (5 cm) of a basal rooting type.

Above: *Lilium columbianum* in Oregon
Below: *Lilium* 'Shuksan' at the Savill gardens

Above: *Lilium pardalinum*
Below: *Lilium martagon*

Above: *Lilium albanicum*
Below: *Lilium pyrenaicum*

For *L. bulbiferum croceum* and *L. bulbiferum* a depth of 5 inches (12 cm) would be sufficient.

The various species of lilies I have seen growing in the wild, include *L. pardalinum* and *L. columbianum*. I found *L. pardalinum* growing on a sunbaked hillside in California. Its versatility is demonstrated by the fact that I also saw the same species growing in the giant redwood forests in the northern part of this state. *L. pardalinum* is a part-parent of the Bellingham hybrids, which do so well at the Savill gardens. *L. columbianum* also has its home in N. America, and I found this high up on a hillside in Oregon. All species seem to enjoy close association with other plants, be they trees or shrubs. These give protection, particularly to the young flowering stems early in the growing season. Then, in due course, the debris of falling leaves forms a protective mulch which rots to enrich the soil.

There is a probability that the Turk's-cap, *L. martagon* is a native of this country. A colony which I saw in Devon some years ago, growing wild in rough grass alongside a copse, looked very much at home. The evidence is by no means conclusive – early writers on the subject describe it as a native of mainland Europe. *L. martagon* is the most widely distributed of all the species, its range extends from Portugal through Europe to Siberia, Turkestan, and Mongolia. As would be expected, the variations in soils over such a wide area must be enormous, and this is reflected in the way *L. martagon* has adapted to garden conditions. They are remarkable in the arrangement of the numerous dark green leaves, usually in the form of whorls round the stem. The flower stem can be anything up to 6 feet (1.8 m) in height. The pendulous flowers with turned-back petals and conspicuously protruding stamens are usually purple, but varieties are available with white, pink, red-purple, and almost black flowers – from three to as many as forty to a stem. Of all the *L. martagon* varieties, those with pure white flowers and dark green foliage are the most pleasing. The roots form at the base of the bulb, so they should be planted no more than 3 to 4 inches (7.5 to 10 cm) deep.

Another species which I find most attractive is *L. albanicum*. As its name suggests, it is to be found in southern Europe. Last year I found it growing on the edge of a pine forest in northern Greece quite near the border with Albania. Standing anything between 2 and 4 feet (0.6 to 1.2 m) high, it carried the most delicate yellow flowers.

Scent, like beauty, is in the nose or eyes of the recipient, for *L. pyrenaicum* and, indeed, *L. martagon* are described as having a foul odour. Possibly because my memories of both these easily cultivated lilies are of seeing them in the most pleasant of circumstances I may be biassed, for the scent to me is pleasant enough. Of the early writers, John Parkinson is the first to depict what he describes as the yellow Turk's-cap, so *L. pyrenaicum* is a late sixteenth- or early seventeenth-century introduction. This is surprising, for an easy-going species, native to the Pyrénées, is almost local when compared to the Madonna lily. Very easy to grow, the base-rooting bulbs planted 4 inches (10 cm) deep soon establish to push up greenish-yellow flowers with brown spots and brilliant orange anthers on stems 3 feet (90 cm) high in June.

The bright orange flowers of the tiger lily, flaunting themselves against the shiny waxen leaves of a laurel hedge in August, were such an accepted part of life's pattern that they conditioned me into thinking of *L. tigrinum* as one of the older species in cultivation. In fact, bulbs were sent to Kew from China in 1804. The Chinese grew them as a farm crop for the sake of the bulbs, which are edible. It is a stem-rooting lily which needs planting 6 inches (15 cm) deep. The orange-red petals curl back to show a purple spotted interior. A form, introduced by Robert Fortune from Korea in 1850, grows taller, with stems covered in a cottony pubescence and bearing from twenty to thirty large flowers.

Lilium longiflorum

Another species from the Far East which has won favour with indoor gardeners is the Easter lily, *L. longiflorum*. This has its origins in Japan. Its long, white, trumpet-shaped flowers and its ability to be forced easily make it a very popular house plant.

In his book *The Lilies of Eastern Asia*, E. H. Wilson, the plant hunter who introduced *L. regale*, writes: 'This lily has a surprisingly limited distribution, being confined to about fifty miles of the narrow semi-arid valley of the Min River in extreme Western Szechuan, between 2500 and 6000 ft [750 and 1800m] altitude – a region where the summers are hot and the winters are cold. From the last week in April to the first week in July, according to altitude the blossoms of this lily transform a desolate, lonely region into a veritable garden of beauty, and its fragrance fills the air.'

Along the valley, according to Wilson's report, the lily is plentiful, growing among grasses and low shrubs. So far as is known at the present time, this wild, lonely valley of the Min river is the only place where *L. regale* grows wild. Mr E. H. Wilson sent home bulbs to the nursery firm of Messrs Vietch in 1904. It was one of the most important plant introductions of his career, for this, one of the loveliest of lilies, has been a major influence in the breeding of new varieties. The slender, flexible, yet strong flower stems grow 3 to 4 feet (0.9 to 1.2 m) tall and are crowned by a number of funnel-shaped blooms. These are shaded brown, fading to pink on the outside, while the inside is yellow in the centre graduating to pure white at the rim. It is a superb lily for the garden – the bulbs can be planted in the autumn or spring, 6 inches (15 cm) deep, as they are stem-rooting. New stock can be grown from seed for flowering in two years, thus amassing large quantities of bulbs for growing in pots, or for general planting.

Though *L. auratum*, the golden-rayed lily of Japan, was brought to this country by Mr J. G. Vietch some forty years before *L. regale* and caused something of a sensation when exhibited, it has not the same sound constitution and perennial qualities. Maybe the plant's immediate popularity led to over-production, for it quickly becomes infected with a weakening

Top right: *Lilium regale*
Below right: *Lilium auratum*

virus disease. In Japan it grows wild in areas ranging from Honshu to the north, and down into Hokkondo in the south west. One form grows in volcanic detritus on the slopes of Mount Fuji Yama – a condition it would be hard to reproduce in a garden. Though *L. auratum* is virus-prone, it has made a most important contribution as a parent of numerous hybrids. Once again, it is Mr E. F. Wilson who, after seeing them growing in the wild, gives the soundest advice on their cultivation. Healthy bulbs planted from 8 to 12 inches (20 to 30 cm) deep in not-too-fertile, lime-free soil where the drainage is perfect and amongst shrubs which protect the young growth from sunlight, will thrive as they do on their native heath. I grew several varieties of *L. auratum* in open woodland amongst azaleas whose roots ensured that no surplus moisture lingered overlong, and they flowered well for eight years. Deep planting is important, as this is a stem-rooting species, and an annual top dressing of leaf-mould will be beneficial. The flowers are large, often 12 inches (30 cm) across, and carried in profusion on tall stems. Ivory white in colour, they are spotted maroon to red and with a distinct gold bar down each petal. Add to the superb flower a fragrance which rejoices the garden from July to October if several varieties are planted, and this lily becomes a paragon of garden plants.

Ranking with the golden-rayed lily in popularity and importance to the plant hybridist, *L. speciosum* is a species of singular charm. Whereas *L. auratum*, in my experience, produces few if any secondary bulbs, *L. speciosum* will establish thriving colonies given the right soil conditions. The native home of *L. speciosum* is given by some authorities as south Japan and, indeed, it is grown extensively in Japanese nurseries, whereas others give the hills of central China as the point of origin. The name *speciosum*, meaning showy or splendid, aptly describes the flamboyant, brilliance of the flowers. One of the latest to come into bloom in northern gardens – September to October – it makes a splendid complement to the autumn colour of maples and Sargent's cherry. Bulbs can be planted in the autumn, or potted up and then moved out in spring. As stem rooters, they need to go down deep, even 8 inches (20 cm) is not too much in well-prepared soil. Widely reflexing flowers which measure 6 inches (15 cm) or more across are carried on 3- to 5-foot (0.9- to 1.5-m) stems. These are a carmine red on an ivory-white background, and they are delightfully but not overpoweringly fragrant. Many varieties exist of this quite variable lily, plus an ever-increasing selection of hybrids. Another attractive and relatively recent addition is *L. mackliniae* from Manipur. This species is easily raised from seed.

One of the best known North American species, *L. canadense* grows in meadows and marshy places – the sort of conditions most gardeners would be reluctant to provide. Bulbs of this most attractive lily, which I planted in moist soil amongst azaleas, increased steadily into a thriving, well-flowered colony. Regular mulching with leaf-mould supplied a sufficiently cool, moist root run. The bulbs are rhizomatous (the new bulb grows on the end of a scaly underground stem) and should be planted 8 inches (20 cm) deep. Bell-shaped flowers which appear on 4- to 5-foot (1.2- to 1.5-m) high stems in June vary in colour from yellow, through orange to red.

There is so much variation in both flower form and colour amongst the species, that exploring all the attributes lends extra interest to the growing of these plants.

Far left: *Lilium mackliniae*
Left: *Lilium monadelphum szovitsianum*

The author in an Oregon bulb field with *Lilium* 'Gold Medal'

From the Caucasus, the amiable *L. monadelphum szovitsianum* is one I have grown for many years, for it is a beautiful form. Stems 5 to 6 feet (1.5 to 1.8 m) high carry from ten to twenty deep yellow, waxy, fragrant flowers which open in June. The bulbs should be planted 5 inches (12.5 cm) deep amongst deciduous shrubs in a west facing border.

Central China has provided so many exceptional species that I am always persuaded to try and accommodate any which come my way. *L. henryi*, sometimes called the orange speciosum, will grow in most soils including those containing lime. Listed as growing only 5 feet (1.5 m) high in the wild, in cultivation it sometimes tops 8 feet (2.4 m) with up to twenty orange-coloured flowers per stem in July and August. It is a stem-rooting species, so the bulbs are planted 6 to 8 inches (15 to 20 cm deep.

Hybridising between the species has resulted in variations which are bewildering in their complexity, and in some cases

aggressively violent in flower colour. The first hybrid was the result of a natural cross-pollination between *L. candidum* and the bright orange-scarlet *L. chalcedonicum* which, surprisingly turned up in a package of *L. martagon* bulbs. The hybrid bloomed in 1838, the dark apricot petals reflexing to show contrasting orange anthers. Called *L. × testaceum*, this is a lovely lily which will tolerate a lime soil. As with *L. candidum*, it is base-rooting, so it should be covered with no more than 2 inches (5 cm) of soil.

The first hybrid was followed by imports from Japan of a race of garden lilies now grouped under *L. × maculatum*, and these are, in my experience, the most tolerant and easily cultivated of all lilies. They are the earliest to flower – in June most years – displaying ample heads of upward facing flowers. The bulbs are large and should be planted 6 to 8 inches (15 to 20 cm) deep where the flower stems can be seen against a dark foliaged shrub. All are compact in height growing up to 3 feet (90 cm) or possibly an inch or two more in good soil. The flowers can be in shades of yellow, orange, or crimson. Most of those I grow are orange-crimson and flower very freely. *L. × hollandicum* includes *L. maculatum* in its parentage, with the same colour range, but with me the flowers open a little later in July.

In recent years, skilful, world-wide cross-pollination has resulted in the introduction of an ever-increasing range of hybrids. The bulb fields of Oregon have yielded robust, floriferous perennials which even the complete gardening novice should find pleasantly easy to grow.

Above:
Lilium 'Impact' (Asiatic)
Top right:
Lilium 'Black Dragon' (Trumpet)
Centre right:
Lilium 'Golden Splendour' (Aurelian)
Below right:
An unnamed hybrid of Dr Chris North

Below: *Lilium chalcedonicum*

'Enchantment' is excellent both in the garden and as a pot plant. A single bulb can produce 30- to 36-inch (75- to 90-cm) high stems with a dozen or more large, bright orange, outward facing flowers – usually in July. 'Edith' is of similar character though with flowers of pale primrose yellow. 'Impact', with flowers of even brighter orange than 'Enchantment', has purple stripes at the base of each petal as if some one had carefully drawn a paint brush across each bloom.

Those with a preference for the spectacularly lovely flared trumpet lilies will possibly find themselves spoiled for choice. 'Golden Splendour' has 6-inch (15-cm) wide blooms, the deep gold petals embellished with a maroon stripe on the outer side. A stem 5 feet (1.5m) high carrying six or more fully open flowers makes a lovely picture in August sunshine. 'Black Dragon' is equally imposing. The flowers 8 inches (20 cm) across are like flared trumpets, white on the inside, maroon on the reverse, with a fragrance that is discernible from a considerable distance. Sturdy stems 6 feet (1.8 m) high may support up to twenty flowers on a well grown plant.

In this country, Dr Chris North from the Invergowie Plant Breeding Research Station in Scotland has made a significant contribution to new, disease-tolerant lilies. Using *L. lankongense* as a parent with embryo culture techniques, he has brought a new dimension to the lily as a garden flower with his attractive hybrids.

Cardiocrinum giganteum

Though no longer a member of the lily genus, *Cardiocrinum giganteum* was for so long the largest and tallest of the clan until botanists ordered its expulsion, that it is only proper to offer it at least a mention. The only difference between this and a true lily is in the broad, heart-shaped leaves which form in whorls near the bottom of the stem. They grow up to 8 feet (2.4 m) high, even 10 feet (3 m) in rich soil, and bear numerous creamy white, fragrant, tubular-shaped flowers. Each individual bloom is at least 6 inches (15 cm) long and is streaked with purple. The flowering season is July and August. The bulbs, which die after flowering, should be planted shallowly in the richest possible soil with the tip exposed on the surface. A heavy mulch of rotted manure or leaf-mould should be spread over the bed to protect the bulbs from frost. Though the parent bulb dies after flowering, offsets form which in due course grow and produce flowers and seed in their turn. To give an indication as to how rich the soil needs to be, one of the tasks I helped with as a gardening apprentice was the preparation of a bed prior to planting *Cardiocrinum giganteum.* The ingredients used included slaughter-house offal, beech leaf-mould, and chopped loam. When the bulbs flowered, each 10-feet (3-m) high stem carried at least twenty blooms.

Lilium 'Midnight' (Aurelian)

Lilium 'Cover Girl' (Oriental)

Lilium × *hollandicum*

The propagation of lilies to increase stock is not difficult. Seed can be sown immediately it is ripe into a frame or into boxes which need to be at least 8 inches (20 cm) deep and filled with loam-based compost. Once germinated, the seed can be left to grow for two years before the small bulbs are transferred to a nursery border.

Lily bulbs are made up of a series of fleshy overlapping 'scales'. If these are detached carefully and inserted into John Innes or peat-based compost, they will grow a new bulb at the base. The process can be shortened if the scales are mixed with peat, then placed in a polythene bag, and hung in a warm, dark place – the airing cupboard is ideal. In six weeks each scale will have grown roots and can then be potted off.

Some of the lilies very obligingly grow small bulbs in leaf axils and amongst the flower heads, *L. tigrinum*, *L.* × *maculatum*, and *L. bulbiferum* are three which do this. These can be removed in early autumn and potted up in loam or a peat-based compost for growing on. Ariel bulbs are known as bulbils, and are not to be confused with bulblets which form at or below soil level. Bulblets appear in many varieties on the underground section of the stem, just above the bulb, and these can also be removed without disturbing the bulb, and potted up.

There are lilies – *L.* × *maculatum*, *L. bulbiferum croceum*, and *L. candidum* which, having had the flower stem pulled from the old bulb as the flowers fade, and being laid in a compost of equal parts loam, peat and sand, will form small bulblets on the stem, usually near where the stem was pulled from the old bulb.

Division is an obvious method of increasing stock, though this is only possible where the lilies are really thriving. Even then I would hesitate to lift established bulbs or disturb them any more than necessary. A few scales can be taken from each bulb without them being lifted, so this is the system I adopt.

Lilies bring a regal quality to the garden which no other flower, not even the rose can equal. Among things lovely and of good report the lily claims a place.

The Lily Group of the Royal Horticultural Society and the North American Lily Society have classified the various hybrid lilies produced from inter-specific hybridisation into eight groups:

1. Asiatics – derived from such species as *L. tigrinum* and *L. davidii* and hybrid groups such as *L.* × *hollandicum* and *L.* × *maculatum*.
2. Martagons – hybrids of *L. martagon* or *L. hansonii* with Turk's-cap flowers.
3. Hybrids derived from *L. candidum*, *L. chalcedonicum* and other related European species, but excluding *L. martagon*.
4. Hybrids of American species.
5. Hybrids derived from *L. longiflorum* and *L. formosanum*.
6. Trumpet-flowered Aurelian hybrids.
7. Orientals – derived from species such as *L. auratum*, *L. speciosum*, *L. japonicum* etc.
8. Hybrids not classified elsewhere.

2
Violas

Most of the world's plants have no common names, they are known only by a botanical or Latin designation. Quite naturally, before a system of botanical nomenclature was devised, country folk contrived names to identify any plant which was of interest, either in economic, medicinal, religious, or aesthetic terms. Sometimes the original, popular name for a plant is incorporated into the botanical title. Occasionally a popular name is adopted from another language. The pansy, known for constancy and remembrance in British folk lore derives from a French word *pensée*, meaning *thought*. Few of our native flowers enjoy the affectionate esteem bestowed on the wild pansy, *Viola tricolor*, and this is reflected in the multiplicity of common names – at the time of writing I have discovered sixteen. My favourites are heart's-ease, kiss-me-at-the-garden-gate, and tittle-my-fancy.

The family is a large one, for over five hundred species are contained within the genus *Viola*. Some are annuals, while

Modern hybrid pansies and a wild violet

Far left: *Viola tricolor*
Left: *Viola odorata* (white form)

others, including the species cultivated as garden plants, are short-lived perennials for the most part. The best known are *V. odorata*, sweet violet, and *V. tricolor* – ancestor of the pansy. The race of hybrids bred from *V. tricolor*, assisted by crosses from other species are grouped for convenience under *Viola* × *wittrockiana*.

Oldest in cultivation is sweet violet which has flowers in shades of purple and white. This was grown for sale as a cut flower in Greek markets four hundred years before the birth of Christ. Ion, the Greek name for the violet, is reputed to have been bestowed on the flower by Jupiter when he changed Io, daughter of the King of Argos with whom he fell in love, into a white heifer, so as to conceal her from the jealousy of his wife Hera. Jupiter then caused sweet violets to spring from the earth, thus providing herbage worthy of her beauty.

In eastern countries the violet, possibly *V. alba* not our native *V. odorata*, enjoys enormous prestige. Sherbet flavoured with the blossom was a popular drink at Arabian banquets. The Persian adage 'The excellence of the violet is as the excellence of El Islam above all other religions', indicates the regard, almost reverence, in which the flower was held. Romans also held violets in high esteem, cultivating them in gardens, and using the flowers to fashion garlands for a favourite poet or bard. The blooms were also used for making wine, a curious competitor, indeed, for the beverage fermented from the grape. In Britain the violet was an emblem of constancy. To quote from an old sonnet 'Violets is for faithfulness, which in me shall abide'.

Violet flowers were much used as a flavouring in confectionery and are still sold coated with sugar and gum arabic as cake decorations. I find it puzzling that the violet was not used in the perfume trade until the very late eighteenth century. Possibly the essence proved difficult to extract and fix, or substances such as orris, made from the rhizome of an iris, offered a cheaper alternative. The violet, along with the rose, was a favourite flower of the Empress Josephine, wife of Napoleon, who cultivated the plants in her famous garden at Malmaison. Roses are still grown in the garden there, though search as I might only one small clump of violets revealed itself growing wild in the shade of trees beside the lake. Violets, their popularity stimulated by royal patronage, were cultivated intensively in gardens near Paris for sale in the city. In southern France violets were grown on a field scale for the perfume which could be extracted from the flowers, and for export to the London market.

In England the growing of violets on a commercial scale was mostly confined to the Avon valley where the flowers were used in the manufacture of a chemical called Syrup of Violets. As their attractiveness as a cut flower grew, nurseries specialising in violet culture began to appear near several major cities, particularly London but also Bath and Bristol.

Though our native sweet violet has been cultivated in gardens for centuries and has given rise to a quantity of natural mutations or 'sports', the modern varieties are the result of crosses between several species. *V. cyanea* from Russia with fragrant blue or violet flowers is one of the 'stud' species.

Below left: *Viola* 'Perle Rose'
Below: *Viola* 'St Helena'

Viola 'Duchesse de Parme'

Another is *V. suavis* which in the wild ranges from Russia through Turkey to Kashmir. I grow this species, or one closely akin to it, as *V. pontica*; it carries large pale blue flowers with a white eye and distills a pleasing fragrance. Last though certainly not least in importance, and again much like sweet violet in appearance, is *V. alba*, with white, violet, and all shades between, including rose and reddish-purple, sweetly-scented flowers. The 'Czar' which has the distinction of being the first violet to gain an award from the Royal Horticultural Society, raised in 1863 at Cranford in Middlesex, was a Russian seedling. Growers from then on introduced a whole range of new hybrids with the 'Czar' as one parent. 'Princess of Wales' with rich violet flowers on long stems, 'St Helena' in pale lavender-blue, 'Perle Rose' and 'Duchesse de Parme' are four notable names from a very long list.

The Parma violets, though they have been grown in this country for over a century are a beautiful, difficult to cultivate

Viola lutea

mystery, whose origins are uncertain. They did, however, achieve an immense popularity with a perfume which once enjoyed is never forgotten, and is, I think, different in the musk rose overtone to that of the sweet violet. I have only been able to grow these under northern conditions in a cold frame; possibly elsewhere they will survive outdoors.

A deep, fertile, well-drained, slightly alkaline soil will usually grow violets well. Before planting it is advisable to dig in a liberal dressing of well-rotted farm manure, compost, or leaf-mould so that the soil is moisture-retentive yet porous enough for the roots to penetrate easily.

Runners or roots may be planted in spring with the crown of the plant just resting fractionally above soil level. Once the roots are established, remove any runners which grow from the centre to concentrate all the plant's energy into flower production.

The popular pansy is, compared to the violet, a native with a well-recorded history. Fortunately, the man who began by hybridisation and selection to improve the flower quality of the garden pansy, *V.* × *wittrockiana*, was that uncommon combination of gardener, plant breeder, and author – a man called Thompson, gardener to Lord Gambier. Starting with the yellow and white heart's-ease about 1814, Mr Thompson began to select those of his raised seedlings which showed improved flower size and colour variation. Encouraged by the results, he gathered together all the varieties in commerce. The annual *V. tricolor*, perennial *V. lutea*, and possibly the Russian species were all entered into the breeding line. As so frequently happens, the first blotched or 'puss-faced' variety appeared as

Right: a modern hybrid pansy

a self-sown seedling growing amongst heathers. This foundling was restored to its rightful place in the pansy yard, and within another fifteen years the new strain had become 'show' flowers. Even the classification was exact, as it must still be today, for exhibition purposes – 'self-coloured' with petals all one shade, though a contrasting eye was acceptable. Other classes included a single ground colour, white or yellow for the lower petals, with the two upper petals of a differing hue. Interest in the pansy quickened with importation from French and Dutch nurseries of a new strain of pansies which were called 'Fancy' to differentiate them from the already admired Show Pansies. In more recent times, selection has given us 'Dream French Giants', which have no face and come in a wide range of colours.

Gardeners are slow to accept change, and almost a decade passed before the new strain achieved acknowledgment. Now, of course, it is the Show Pansy which is the laggard in popularity. Crosses between *V. lutea*, *V. tricolor*, *V. amoena*, and in the last quarter of the nineteenth century *V. cornuta*, combined to give both garden and bedding pansies a quality which would have delighted Mr Thompson, the man they called 'Father of the heart's-ease'. The description applied to pansies then is still true today. They are inexpensive, easily managed, and beautiful. Botanists group viola, tufted pansy, and violettas (derived from crossing garden pansies with *V. cornuta*) under the title *V.* × *williamsi* – *V.* × *wittrockiana* covers the garden pansy.

The cultivation of the summer flowering varieties, 'Clear Crystal', 'Prince Henry', 'Giant', and 'Roggli' strains, plus the named varieties of tufted pansy, old favourites like 'Maggie Mott' and 'Irish Molly', is similar. A good, fertile, well-drained soil which will not become excessively dry in summer or wet in

Top and above:
'Dream French Giant' pansies

Opposite
Top: *Viola* 'Prince Henry'
Centre: *Viola cornuta*
Below: *Viola biflora*

winter, and sunny or partially shaded borders will suit all varieties. Seed sown in July will produce plants large enough to go outside in their flowering positions by September. Alternatively, seed may be sown under glass in March for planting outdoors in May. All the species and varieties can be propagated by cuttings made from non-flowering basal shoots during the summer months.

Though the species do not enjoy the universal acclaim of the larger-flowered, brighter-coloured hybrids, several are very worthy of garden cultivation. *V. cornuta*, mentioned previously as playing an important part as progenitor of the pansy cum viola, was introduced from the Pyrenees late in the eighteenth century. Conditions in some areas have proved so congenial that it has escaped to become naturalised. The large pale violet flowers open on 10-inch (25-cm) high stems, but there is a white form which occurs naturally when fresh stock is raised from seed. It is an excellent ground cover plant flowering in early summer, then again in early July if the clusters are trimmed with shears. A variety of *V. cornuta* which I grow, called 'Campanula Blue', has lavender-coloured flowers and is a prime perennial.

Another alpine favourite is *V. biflora* with clear, yellow flowers and kidney-shaped leaves. It peeps brightly from beneath and between rocks where it finds sufficient shelter. Much more of a challenge to the gardener's skill is *V. jaubertiana*, which I find does best in an alpine trough.

Some of the species are very tiny, but their elfin charm hides a cast-iron durability. *V. saxatilis aetolica*, or as some catalogues list it – just plain *V. aetolica*, only grows to 2 or 3 inches (5 to 8 cm) high. The pansy-like yellow flowers measure an inch (2.5 cm) across in the best forms. I have grown it amongst dwarf, blue-blossomed rhododendrons which flowered with the viola in April and May. Of the viola species I have grown, *V. cucullata* from North America is one of the most excellent perennials. Heart-shaped, pale green leaves provide the backcloth to inch-wide flowers, varying in shade from white through violet to lavender. *V. beckwithii*, a North American species from Oregon, has two violet upper petals and three lilac lower petals – an ideal natural complement.

There is a tendency for some of the species to be so overshadowed by their more aggressively coloured offspring that they are lost to cultivation, and *V. gracilis* is such a one. I grew my plants from seed, and used them as ground cover over bulbs and hardy cyclamen in a frame. The purple flowers opened in March through to June in a pleasant association with those of bulbs. The species *V. glabella* that I found growing in woodland at the Chelsea Physic Garden in London came originally from the west of North America. In dappled sunlight it seemed to reflect all the delicate charm of the family.

Some species are capable of growing in shady places under trees or on the north side of buildings, and *V. labradorica* is useful in this respect. I grow the form with purple foliage as ground cover in a shade border in company with ferns, dog's-tooth violet and similar plants. There, this viola from North America and Greenland makes a carpet of foliage, starred in spring with mauve flowers borne on 4-inch (10-cm) high stems. When well suited it can be invasive, demanding more than a fair share of space. As would be expected, seed forms the easiest means of raising fresh stock.

Meeting a plant on its own native heath tends to leave an indelible imprint on the memory. Seeing the common dog violet, *V. riviniana* growing in company with primroses on the steeply sloping bank of a stream on a Yorkshire fellside made a lasting impression on my mind. The carpet of violet flowers with primroses growing amongst them, and the soft greenness of spring lying overall had a wild, captivating beauty. Another lasting memory is of *V. canina* growing on a bank in the grounds of Rievaulx Abbey.

Viola jaubertiana

Below left: *Viola beckwithii*
Below: *Viola glabella*

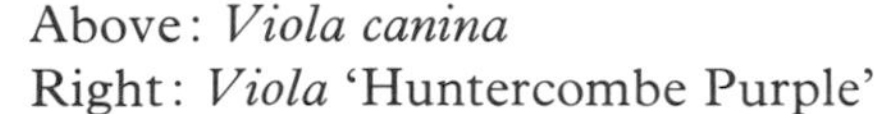

Above: *Viola canina*
Right: *Viola* 'Huntercombe Purple'

V. zoysii is another native I took a liking to when walking in the east European Alps. It has dark foliage and clear yellow flowers.

Were it not so lovely, the bird's-foot violet, *V. pedata* would be dismissed as too difficult and temperamental. I have found it quite content when planted in very sandy soil over a bed of leaf-mould, once the slugs have been persuaded to refrain from devouring it. There, the light blue violet flowers opened in succession during late April and May on 4-inch (10-cm) stems.

Though the mountain pansy, *V. lutea*, is ancestor to many garden hybrids, it is also one of the prettiest of our native flowers and as such warrants more than just a passing mention. I have seen hillsides where the grass was bejewelled with mountain pansy flowers, mostly yellow, but with a proportion of blue forms, and others a mixture of the two colours. For garden purposes, of course, the hybrids are better value, though I cherish a small colony for the memories the flowers conjure up.

V. tricolor, the little yellow and dark blue flowered annual, known as heart's-ease, seeds itself cheerfully around the garden into any cranny which offers root hold. In poor soils it is neat and compact at only 2 inches (5 cm) high, but given more fertile root run it spreads luxuriantly into a mat 15 inches (38 cm) across and up to 8 inches (20 cm) high.

Hybrids of the pansy derived from *V. tricolor* show their origins if allowed to seed about the garden. Each succeeding generation reverts more nearly to the parent characteristics. There is a subspecies of *V. tricolor*, called *macedonica*, which will grace any garden. Like the species, it flowers all summer through, but its petals are a cheerful dark red. Though only a short-lived annual, self-sown seedlings spring up to fill the space left vacant.

The generous family of violets offers so much choice to the gardener that it is churlish not to provide them bed and board in return for the pleasure they give.

Viola riviniana

3
Fuchsias

Of the hundred or so species of fuchsia identified at the present time ninety-four are natives of Central and South America, four grow naturally in New Zealand, and one grows wild in Tahiti. The genus is named after Leonhard Fuchs, a German professor, physician, and herbalist, whose great work was a book on medicinal plants illustrated with beautiful woodcuts.

Although to the layman's eye there is no similarity between the plants, in their botanical classification fuchsias are grouped in the same family as the evening primrose, willow herb, and godetia. In 1693 Charles Plumier, a French missionary and botanist, discovered on San Domingo a plant he called *Fuchsia triphylla flore coccineo*. In a book he published during 1703, Plumier describes and illustrates the fuchsia he discovered ten years previously. The genus was founded and given botanical classification by Linnaeus in 1753 on the information provided by Father Plumier.

Seeds of the newly discovered fuchsia were sent to Philip Miller, curator of the Chelsea Physic Garden, from Cartagena in Colombia by Dr Houstoun, a Scottish surgeon, who collected plants in Central America and the West Indies. Dr Houstoun also made notes and drawings of the plants he found, so the event is well recorded. Precisely when the seeds were sent is not clear, but as Miller was not made curator until 1722, and Dr Houstoun died in 1733 it must have been during that period.

Fuchsia triphylla is described as a semi-shrubby plant growing from 10 to 20 inches (25 to 50 cm) high with leathery copper-bronze leaves. The flowers have a long, cinnabar-red tube fading at the base, and short petals. As would be expected, *F. triphylla* cannot survive frost or winter temperatures below 40°F. (4°C.). This probably explains why it soon disappeared from cultivation and was not mentioned or seen again, in garden terms that is, for more than a hundred years.

The next recorded species to be found, *F. coccinea*, was again discovered by a French missionary, R. Feuillée, who described it in his book on Chilean plants first published in 1714. The Royal Botanic Gardens at Kew were presented with a plant of *F. coccinea* in 1788 by Captain Firth. There is some difference of opinion amongst writers on the history of the

Fuchsia 'Gartenmeister Bonstedt'

Left: *Fuchsia coccinea*

fuchsia as to whether seed of *F. triphylla* was grown to flowering from the 1722–33 introductions. In the event that the attempt failed, then *F. coccinea* was the first species to be seen growing in this country. Described as a slender branched shrub up to 3 feet (90 cm) in height, it has solitary flowers borne in the upper leaf axils, with a red tube and sepals complemented by a violet to purple corolla. Though the true species is now rare in cultivation, it is of considerable importance having had a major influence in the breeding of new fuchsia hybrids.

Almost at the same time, possibly brought in on the same ship that delivered *F. coccinea*, came *F. magellanica*, adding the first hint of mystery and romance to the fuchsia story. The tale runs that James Lee, a nurseryman of Hammersmith, was showing a prospective customer around his stock, and the visitor, seemingly unimpressed, passed a comment that he had

Left: *Fuchsia magellanica* 'Alba'
Above: *Fuchsia magellanica* in the west coast of Ireland

seen a better plant growing in the window of a house in Wapping. James Lee reacted to this unsolicited piece of information quite predictably by rushing off in search of this paragon of plants, and discovered it to be a fuchsia different to any he had seen. According to the lady, her sailor husband had brought it back from the West Indies. By emptying his pockets of all the cash he had on him, Lee persuaded the woman to part, somewhat reluctantly, with her plant. So, for a total of about eight guineas and a promise that she should also have two of the first cuttings propagated, the woman gave up the prize. The plant, at first wrongly identified as *F. coccinea*, was in truth *F. magellanica*. Fittingly, there is a good plant *F. magellanica* 'Alba' on display at the Chelsea Physic Garden in London.

Those less romantically inclined cast grave doubts on the story. Neither *F. coccinea* or *F. magellanica* is native to the West Indies. Did Lee receive it from one of his own collectors? Did he, as some suggest, invent the story to cover up the acquisition of cuttings from Kew Gardens to account for its being in his possession. No one can now discern truth from fiction. One thing is certain, that in 1793 Lee sold large numbers of fuchsias at considerable profit to himself – reports say the charge was one guinea per plant – a handsome sum indeed.

F. magellanica is native to Chile and Argentina, and is a tall-growing hardy shrub with graceful flowers of the elegant, classic form beloved by the specialists. The colour of bloom is described as tube red, sepals deep red, and corolla purple. In spite of all the stories surrounding its introduction, botanical sources insist there is no evidence of the species being grown in Great Britain prior to 1820. In the wild state *F. magellanica* grows in moist, sometimes marshy ground, which is confirmed by the preference shown in cultivation for areas of high rainfall. In Ireland, the Isle of Man and in Cornwall, hedges of *F.*

Right: *Fuchsia thymifolia* in Mexico

magellanica grow 8 feet (2.4 m) or more in moist, humid conditions. Being hardy, a trait passed on frequently to its offspring, *F. magellanica* is an important stud plant to the hybridist.

In 1827 *F. thymifolia* arrived from Mexico and the next fifty years saw, if not a flood of new introductions, at least what could be described as a constant trickle. *F. lycioides*, brought at the beginning of the nineteenth century from Chile, is a 9-foot (2.7-m) high shrub and fairly hardy, the flower colour – tube red, petals purple. About the same time *F. decussata*, *F. corymbiflora*, *F. apetala* and *F. serratifolia* put in an appearance. Both *F. serratifolia* and *F. corymbiflora* have been used as parents to produce new hybrids. In 1841 *F. splendens* was introduced. In all, fourteen or more species were introduced in the short span of twenty years. Another was *F. microphylla* from Brazil with short stems up to 3 feet (90 cm) high and small dark red and rose

Fuchsia splendens

flowers. Three years later the tree-like *F. arborescens* arrived, a native of Mexico and Panama. A variable plant, which grows sometimes as an epiphyte, a small shrub or, as the name suggests, a 25-foot (7.5-m) high tree, the flowers are not large, the tube is rose, and the corolla lilac. In Mexico I found only one bush, presumed to be *F. arborescens*, scrambling feebly amongst coarse vegetation. One that does grow in profusion in that country is *F. encliandra* which enjoys the conditions that a pine forest can offer.

These lesser members of the genus preceded the arrival of a truly noteworthy member of the family in the shape of *F. fulgens*. Sent from Mexico to the Horticultural Society in 1828, the long tubular flowers and beautiful foliage attracted immediate attention. To see a 4-foot (1.2-m) high specimen growing on a rock outcrop in open woodland with the vast panorama of the Mexican mountains beyond was an unforgettable experience. The leaves were broader than I have seen on any of the many *F. fulgens* which have graced my gardening life. The flowers were larger, bright red and fading to orange at the base. Individuals were scattered across the half mile of hillside which I explored, some interlaced with sub-shrubs, others growing alone in humus-rich, stony soil. There were differences in leaf size and flower colour which seemed to depend more on habitat than genetic variation. *F. fulgens* is reported in the Botanical Magazine for 1841 as being, in combination with other species, the means of producing a great number of hybrids. Curtis of Glazenwood, and Bunney of Stratford were two of the early practitioners in the field.

F. procumbens is a reputedly hardy species which has proved distinctly tender in my experience. It is a most unfuchsia-like prostrate creeping shrub with wiry stems, furnished with heart-shaped leaves. The flowers are small without petals, and they have an orange-yellow calyx tube and purple leaf-like lobes. The fruit, which is the same size as the flowers, colours flesh pink. In its native New Zealand, *F. procumbens* grows in sandy or gravelly soil in coastal regions. A most unusual species, and worth a place in the collection, but I can find no record of New Zealand species hybridising with any others. The cross-fertilising has all been between *F. magellanica*, *F. coccinea*, *F. fulgens* and available species from America.

The earliest break in colour occurred in the mid-nineteenth century, when a seedling from *F. magellanica* flowered showing a white tube and bluish purple corolla. Introduced by a Tunbridge Wells Nursery as 'Venus Victrix', it offered the prospect of new, even more diverse colour variations.

In a very short space of time the fuchsia achieved a remarkable popularity, with breeders in both Great Britain and the continent of Europe, raising seedlings bred from crosses between the available species that were suitably compatible. The first book dealing entirely with fuchsia cultivation was printed in 1848 and lists 520 species and varieties. By the end of the century the number had risen to 1500, and plants were being sold in Covent Garden at the rate of 10,000 per day. One

Above: *Fuchsia arborescens*
Right: *Fuchsia fulgens* in Mexico

Below: *Fuchsia encliandra*

grower, and an amateur at that, is reported as raising 6000 seedlings annually, so it is no wonder that there were so many sorts on offer.

These, so-called, florists' fuchsias are too tender to survive a winter outdoors in this country, though they are used extensively for summer bedding. Instead, credit must be given to the one species, *F. magellanica* and its forms, for the race of shrubs which, even under the extremes of weather conditions inflicted on those who garden in Yorkshire Dales, have proved indestructibly hardy. From the books I have read dealing with the parentage of modern fuchsia hybrids, the two most important species are *F. fulgens* and *F. magellanica*, though other species have contributed and, no doubt, will do so increasingly in the future.

The garden fuchsias, as opposed to those which need winter protection in a greenhouse, make no great demands on the skills of those who grow them. In mild areas the hardy fuchsias make quite large, well-furnished shrubs; elsewhere top growth is frequently killed back to soil level by frost. In spring when all the dead stems are cut away, strong shoots grow from the perennial root to flower in July.

Any well drained soil will suit fuchsias. Before planting, a little rotted leaf soil, compost, or farm manure can be worked into the top twelve inches (30 cm), plus a dusting of meat and bone meal. As fuchsias root very quickly and easily from cuttings of young, non-flowering shoots taken at any time during the growing season, raising extra stock presents no problems.

Above left: *Fuchsia* 'Alice Hoffman'
Above: *Fuchsia* 'Corallina'
Below: *Fuchsia magellanica* 'Riccartonii'

Without doubt *F. magellanica* and varieties derived from it are the hardiest. In the type plant, the flowers though small are carried in such profusion that their individual size becomes unimportant. There was an enormous bush in the garden around my childhood home, and popping the tight buds to make them open became a habit in which I still absentmindedly indulge.

A pale-flowered form called *F. magellanica molinae* is the tallest I have grown, but the pale lilac petals and white tube are too insipid for my taste. There is a form of the dark red-flowered *F. magellanica gracilis* which offers a pleasant alternative to the plain-leaved sort, called 'Variegata'. The red flowers are identical with those of *F. magellanica gracilis*, but are displayed against silver foliage. Any branches which revert to plain green should be pruned away immediately they appear. Of the various forms which are not produced from crosses between *F. magellanica* and another species, *F.m.* 'Riccartonii' is the most planted, particularly as a hedging shrub. The growth is upright while the flowers, carried in generous quantities over many weeks, are particularly colourful – the corolla deep purple and the tube scarlet.

For twenty years I experimented with varieties which offered the prospect of being hardy. With most of the hybrids tried, good drainage frequently made the difference between a plant surviving or being killed by frost. Poor drainage is a curse and abomination to all the fuchsia clan; those not killed outright become pale reflections of similar plants grown on well drained soil. The garden where the fuchsias were grown lies 600 feet (180 m) above sea level in North Yorkshire and, though the trials were limited in scope, they were conclusive enough to convince me that many hardy varieties are ornamental plants not being employed to full advantage as permanent garden features.

'Alice Hoffman', with semi-double flowers, white in the corolla with a rose-pink tube and sepals, is neat and very compact. 'Corallina' introduced in 1845, and so one of the older hybrids now in cultivation, is excellent. I grew it trained to cover a south-facing potting shed, but it is seen to best effect as a free-growing shrub. The purple-tinged foliage is carried on elegantly arching stems. No variety flowers so profusely; the single blooms are scarlet and purple, and lovely when grown with deep blue lavender.

Another long-cultivated form, *F. magellanica globosa*, still holding a place if it came to me correctly named, made a compact, spreading shrub which was an excellent companion to the dark purple autumn-flowering *Crocus speciosus*. The flowers, which do not open to reflex as is usual, were like crimson and purple Chinese lanterns arranged along the stems. 'Genii' is an attractively foliaged very vigorous hybrid spreading in three years into a bush one yard (90 cm) across. The leaves, which are yellowish-green, set off the cerise and violet flowers to good advantage. This variety survived the hard winters of 1963 and 1981, but all top growth was cut to soil level.

Fuchsia 'Tom Thumb'

'Lena' spreads outwards rather than growing up, so it needs more space than most. Introduced in 1862, it has proved to be one of the toughest and most resilient. The semi-double blooms are flesh pink tinged with white, and with a mauve corolla. 'Margaret' is a most flamboyant 1949 introduction which reached 4 feet (1.2 m) high after a succession of mild winters; the semi-double corolla is violet in colour, the tube scarlet. Restricted to only one fuchsia, for good natured reliability after long association I would choose 'Mrs Popple', first grown in 1899. In most gardens it makes a shrub 4 feet (1.2 m) high. The tube of the flowers is a succulent soft crimson and the corolla violet, with the foliage a proper complement.

For the garden where space is at a premium there is a choice which includes 'Tom Thumb', 10 inches (25 cm) high, in carmine and purple, or a sport from this variety, also with semi-double flowers which are coloured light carmine and white. Where age takes precedence, then *F. magellanica* 'Pumila', 6 inches (15 cm) high and introduced in 1821, must be the choice with single flowers of bright red and mauve. Grown inter-

Right: *Fuchsia* 'Lena'
Far right: *Fuchsia* 'Mrs Popple'

mingled with the blue spikes of *Satureja montana* which is of similar height, dwarf fuchsias make a particularly pleasing composition.

Anyone fortunate enough to own a heated greenhouse will find the choice of varieties sufficient to satisfy the most selective gardener. The only certain way of making a selection is to visit a specialist show or nursery, or both. Fuchsias are capable of being trained into a variety of shapes which in their different ways show the beauty and quality of the flowers to best effect. This applies to plants grown in the garden or those cultivated in pots. Some form of pruning and training of the branch framework is essential to produce a well-flowered plant.

The bush form is the simplest, here the number of stems is restricted to what best suits the variety in hand. With some, three stems are sufficient, others will comfortably support six. Side shoots are stopped at two leaves, until the flowering framework is established.

The spherical or ball-head needs more attention. Only varieties which produce long-arching growth respond to this sort of training. By stopping shoots which form in the middle of the plant and training the outside branches to arch over and down, a very beautiful presentation is arrived at.

Standards and half standards are only possible with strong vigorous fuchsias, as the length of clean stem needed before the flowering head is formed can be anything from 18 to 42 inches (45 to 105 cm).

Espaliers and fan-trained forms are even more demanding of time and meticulous skill. For an espalier or fan the branch system is arranged so as to leave a short stem exposed for 2 or 3 inches (5 to 7 cm). The espalier is built up of branches trained out horizontally at intervals up the main stem. Ideally, these should be arranged opposite to each other on a flat plane left and right, but not all the way round.

Fuchsia 'Achievement'

The fan is, as the name implies, made up of a series of branches trained to form a triangular shape.

Varieties of fuchsia with lax or pendulous growth are best grown in hanging baskets. The most widely used for the purpose are 'Marinka', 'Golden Marinka', 'Cascade', and 'Falling Stars'.

To start a general collection, I would choose:

'Achievement' which, though a hundred years old, is easy to grow and train to most shapes. The flowers are cerise and purple.

'The Aristocrat', white, pink and pale rose is equal to any other in vigour and trainability.

'Aurora Superba', slim with 5 inch (12.5 cm) long flowers.

'Bon Accorde', again an old variety of stiff upright growth with purple and white flowers.

'Citation' makes good half-standards, rose pink and white.

'Dollar Princess', a real beginner's plant, cerise and purple.

'Glitter', long elegant flowers with delicate pink sepals and red tube.

'Lovable' because the colour combination is so lovely.

'Pink Jade', with delicate pink flowers.

'Snowcap' is an easily trained bush form with semi-double flowers in red and white.

'Swing Time', which responds to most styles and shaping, has double blooms coloured red and ivory white.

'Tennessee Waltz', a single rose-pink and lilac, made the best standard I have ever grown, with the least trouble.

'White Spider' with attractive white flowers. Ideal for a hanging basket or archway.

Golden foliaged varieties:

'Carl Drude' with red and white flowers.

'Gilda' golden green foliage, red and pink flowers.

Below left: *Fuchsia* 'Marinka'
Below: *Fuchsia* 'White Spider'

Top right: *Fuchsia* 'Falling Stars'
Right: *Fuchsia* 'Pink Jade'

Below: *Fuchsia* 'Swing Time'
Below right: *Fuchsia* 'Bon Accorde'

4
Peonies

The peony, according to ancient folk lore, drives away tempests and dispels enchantments, so in garden terms it is a plant both useful and beautiful. From early times the peony was held in high regard for its powers of healing. The name itself suggests this, being derived from Paeon, first physician of the Gods, who used peony root to cure Pluto of the wound inflicted on him by Hercules. In this country necklaces of beads made from peony root were worn by young children to help them in teething and as a protection against epileptic fits. The medicinal reputation is no longer acknowledged except in Chinese traditional medicine. Instead, the plant is valued on account of its ornamental flowers.

Until recently the genus *Paeonia* was placed in the same family as the buttercup, the Ranunculaceae. The flowers do show a similarity. Now it is separated from Ranunculaceae in a class of its own, the Paeoniaceae. Modern selections apart, the peony is an ancient plant in cultivation, particularly in terms of Chinese and Japanese gardening history.

Paeonia are mostly herbaceous perennials, apart from four species which develop a woody, shrub-like character, and are distinguished from the common herd by the popular name tree peony. *Paeonia delavayi* makes a deciduous shrub up to 6 feet (1.8 m) high, and is one of the hardiest. A handsome shrub with single flowers opening in May, the deep red petals are in bright contrast to the central cluster of yellow stamens. Seed is ripened most years, and this offers a simple way of raising fresh stock, if sown immediately the pod splits in the autumn. *P. delavayi* will grow in any reasonably fertile garden soil, and in every respect it is a most amiable shrub.

The plant was first discovered by the Abbé Delavay in the province of Yunnan in China, sometime during the ten years he was stationed at the mission there. Unfortunately, many of the boxes of plants which Delavay sent to Paris lay unopened for many years. So it was not until an English plant hunter, E. H. Wilson, sent seeds back to this country that *P. delavayi* was effectively brought under cultivation early in the present century. What is curious, is that Wilson had been sent out to China by the nursery firm of Veitch to collect the seeds of

Paeonia delavayi at the Royal Botanic Garden, Kew

Davidia involucrata, the pocket handkerchief tree, and nothing else. The seeds of 305 different plant species, plus thirty-five cases of bulbs and live roots which Wilson also collected were merely incidental acquisitions which were to prove of immense benefit to gardeners.

The slightly dwarfer *P. lutea* was also discovered and, unlike *P. delavayi*, was actually introduced by the Abbé Delavay during his term in Yunnan about the year 1887. The flowers are 2½ inches (6 cm) across, slightly more in the better forms, with golden yellow petals. Indeed, in the variety *ludlowii* (introduced in 1936), which flowers earlier in May than the

Paeonia lutea ludlowii

type species, individual blooms can reach 5 inches (13 cm) in diameter. Growing as it does naturally at elevations of up to 11,000 feet (3300 m) *P. lutea* in all its forms is hardy in most gardens throughout the British Isles. Seed offers the best method of raising new plants.

The most important of the tree peonies is, undoubtedly, *P. suffruticosa* both in historical and garden terms. In wild plants the white-petalled, maroon or scarlet-centred blooms measure 6 inches (15 cm) across. The fragrance of these flowers, which open in May to June, is quite pleasant. The same cannot be said for some of the hybrids. A native of northern China, the moutan, *P. suffruticosa,* is now rarely found in a wild state. In Chinese gardens, however, the history of its cultivation goes back many centuries to when the first plants were introduced into the Imperial gardens during the seventh century AD. By the tenth century thirty-nine varieties were on sale. These varieties were propagated by grafting scions onto rootstocks of the wild species. 'Rock's Variety' is an attractive garden form with white petals and a large maroon blotch in the centre of the single or semi-double flowers.

The early introductions to Europe came from Canton, one of the areas visited by Robert Fortune, who was to make some interesting observations on the plants and people of China. Fortune noted that in Canton thousands of moutan peonies were imported each year from northern China. The popular Chinese name for the plant, moutan, roughly translated, means 'male vermilion'.

The moutan came to this country through the efforts of Sir Joseph Banks, who was keen to have specimens of such a

Paeonia lutea

Paeonia suffruticosa hybrid at Walpole House Garden in London

Paeonia suffruticosa 'Rock's Variety'

desirable plant growing in Kew Gardens. He engaged a Mr Duncan who was in service with the East India Company to send plants to England. The first consignment arrived at Kew Gardens in 1787. Robert Fortune made his first expedition to China just over fifty years later, his plants went to the Horticultural Society's gardens, and proved to be hybrids with almost fully double flowers. Reginald Farrer, of alpine fame, was one of the fortunate few to have seen *P. suffruticosa* growing wild, in 1914 near Kaichow. Farrer waxed lyrical as only he could on 'the huge expanded goblets of Paeonia Moutan, refulgent as pure snow, and fragrant as heavenly roses'. Unfortunately, *P. suffruticosa* and its many cultivars is not predictably easy to grow. In the wild it enjoys complete winter dormancy, a resting period forced on it by quite severe frost and snow. This probably explains why the best specimens I know are growing in Yorkshire gardens where there is less danger of their being persuaded into precocious growth, only to have shoots and flower buds killed by late frost. A well-cultivated soil and a position facing north-west will suit the moutan. Annual mulching with rotted manure, leaf-mould or compost is a further subscription to ensure continued well-being of this lovely tree peony.

Propagation of the cultivars is usually by grafting onto either seedling *P. suffruticosa* or varieties of herbaceous peony.

How very easy it would be in considering the charms of tree peonies to overlook the qualities of the herbaceous species. In the final analysis they are more accommodating garden plants – they have lovely flowers, attractive foliage, and seed pods which in some species split open to reveal brightly-coloured seeds.

Paeonia mascula at Steep Holme

The first of the species known in this country was *P. mascula*, the male peony, arguably a native, more probably a feral monastry garden escape which grew wild near Winchcombe in the Cotswolds and Steep Holme in the Bristol Channel. A perennial between 18 and 24 inches (45 to 61 cm) high, with dark green leaves and deep red flowers 4 inches (10 cm) in diameter. There is a form from southern Europe and Asia Minor called *P. mascula arietina*. The plant I grew had leaves with a greyish down on the undersides, and beautiful cup-shaped flowers of rose-pink. *P. officinalis* is the female peony from the Mediterranean coast. I believe the names male and female are a legacy from the time when peonies were grown as medicinal plants. *P. mascula* or male peony was specific against disorders affecting men, *P. officinalis* or female peony was used for women's ailments.

Certainly, in 1548 *P. officinalis* was described by gardening writers of the time as common throughout England, presumably in gardens and not as a wild plant, either natural or feral. Hybrids derived from this species include some of the oldest and best loved of garden peonies. The old double-red 'Rubra Plena' is a particular favourite of mine, for it was the first of the clan of which I was aware. 'Rosea Superba Plena' is of a light-pink shade. Amongst the singles, 18 inch (45 cm) high 'China Rose', with cupped salmon-pink petals opening to reveal orange stamens, would be hard to improve on.

There is a surprisingly large number of plants which to all intents and purposes have become accepted through long association as British; *P. lactiflora* is one. Though this species was brought to this country two hundred years ago from Siberia, the Chinese had been growing and admiring it for a thousand years before that. The first importation died, so Sir Joseph Banks procured fresh stock from China early in the nineteenth century. This species is parent to many of the brightly coloured, sweetly fragrant Chinese peonies brought from China in those times. Another fifty years were to pass before James Kelway raised the hybridisation of peonies to new

Paeonia mascula arietina

Above: *Paeonia officinalis* at Kew
Right: *Paeonia lactiflora* 'Superba'

levels, producing a whole range of home-grown cultivars.

A native of Siberia, Mongolia, and northern China, *P. lactiflora* was valued as a medicinal plant. The Mongols made a soup of the roots, and used the powdered seeds to flavour tea.

There are many cultivars which owe at least some characteristic to *P. lactiflora*: 'Whitleyi Major' and 'The Bride' are two, with white, sweetly-scented flowers. Others include 'Superba', single off-white petals cupping yellow stamens; 'Sarah Bernhardt', double rose-purple petals edged with pink; and 'La France', single and semi-double rich rose-pink. In the type species, however, the flowers are white and sweetly-scented; they measure 4 inches (10 cm) across and are carried on 18-inch (45-cm) high stems during early June.

Any good garden soil that is well-cultivated and fertile will suit these plants, usually referred to as Chinese peonies. The roots are best left undisturbed. Soil fertility can be maintained with a dressing of fertiliser in late winter, together with a mulch of rotted manure or compost.

P. emodi is tall, up to 3 feet (90 cm) in height, and is found growing wild in the Northern Provinces of India. The golden stamened, white-petalled flowers have a pleasing scent. In my experience *P. emodi* is happier in partial shade. The shrub roses provide just the right amount of protection in this respect.

Inevitably, amongst the clan there has to be one member favoured above all others and, in spite of the name, *P. mlokosewitschii* has top place with me. The name is easy to remember if anglicised to 'Mock the Witch's Eye'. A native of the Caucasus, this species was introduced quite recently – during the first decade of this century. Always the first of the genus *Paeonia* to flower, in May, it is beautiful in all parts. The broad grey-green leaves provide the loveliest complement to the large lemon-yellow flowers. Then, in the late summer, the seed capsule splits to add a further distinction with red and black seeds. Compared to the other species at only 15 to 18 inches (38 to 45 cm) high, 'Mock the Witch's Eye' is a dwarf, though like the other new plants is easily raised from seed.

Paeonia mlokosewitschii

Left: *Paeonia clusii* on a Cretan mountainside
Top: *Paeonia parnassica* in Greece
Above: *Paeonia obovata*

Though *P. obovata* is a native of Siberia and China, it expresses a profound dislike of the bitter east winds which are such a familiar experience in spring. Only in the warmest, most sheltered corners will this very beautiful peony thrive. There, the grey-green, copper-tinted leaves arch over to reveal 18-inch (45-cm) high flower spikes which each support one pure white-petalled, golden-centred bloom. I have never seen the flower any other colour but white, so I can only offer Henry Ford's choice 'of any colour providing it is white'. The soil needs to be enriched with leaf-mould, and a mulch of the same material every spring will seduce *P. obovata* into an extended association. For a long time I have searched for the form with pale primrose-coloured blooms known as 'Willmottiae' which I saw growing in a Devon garden. Like the Holy Grail of the Crusaders it continues to elude me. But one peony which did not elude me was *P. clusii*. I found it growing on a stony hillside in Crete last year. The solitary white flowers were a pure delight. Two others, less well known perhaps, which have their home in that particular part of the world are *P. parnassica* (southern Greece) and *P. mascula hellenica*, the latter's name matching its natural beauty.

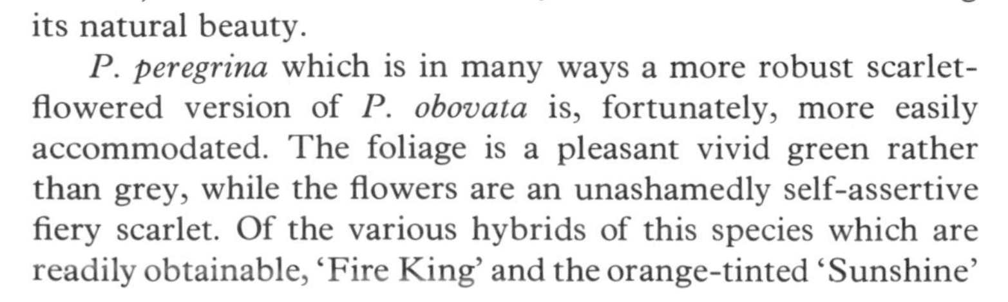

P. peregrina which is in many ways a more robust scarlet-flowered version of *P. obovata* is, fortunately, more easily accommodated. The foliage is a pleasant vivid green rather than grey, while the flowers are an unashamedly self-assertive fiery scarlet. Of the various hybrids of this species which are readily obtainable, 'Fire King' and the orange-tinted 'Sunshine'

Paeonia mascula hellenica on a Greek hillside

Top: *Paeonia tenuifolia*
Above: *Paeonia veitchii woodwardii* 'Alba'
Right: *Paeonia tenuifolia* (pink form)

Below: *Paeonia humilis*

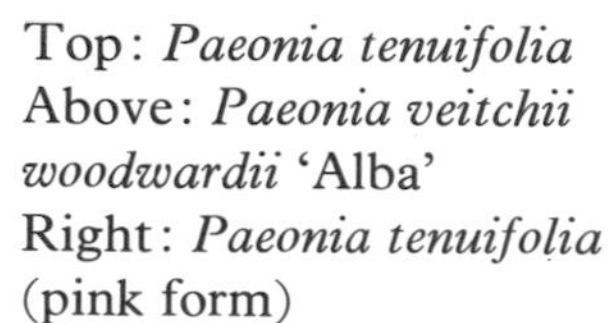

are good examples. In fertile, well-drained, heavy loam it reaches about 24 inches (60 cm) or slightly less on a soil which dries out rapidly under summer sunshine.

There are two species which would not be out of character when planted amongst dwarf shrubs on the outskirts of a large rock garden. *P. tenuifolia* is one, *P. veitchii* the other. *P. tenuifolia* is a Caucasian which was introduced to this country only forty years after *P. officinalis*, so it is no brash newcomer to our gardens. The leaves are so finely divided as to form a lacy Elizabethan ruff to the flowers. Of the two plants I have grown, both called *P. tenuifolia*, one had dark crimson, cup-shaped blooms, the other had deep pink. Both were equipped with a central boss of yellow stamens and grew no more than 16 inches (40 cm) high.

The second rock garden candidate *P. veitchii*, when satisfied with the accommodation offered, produces self-sown seedlings as an expression of gratitude. Only the largest, best coloured forms need be retained. Growing only 1 foot (30 cm) high, this neat Chinese species is, compared to *P. tenuifolia*, very much the new boy. It was brought to Britain during the first decade of the present century. A happy little plant with attractive mid-green leaves, and single, modestly nodding flowers which have petals of deep magenta. For those who find magenta unpleasant, the variety *P. veitchii woodwardii* 'Alba' offers an alternative. *P. humilis* is another low-growing species with red flowers and the attractive feature of dense hairs growing on the underside of the leaves.

Paeonia cambessedesii

P. cambessedesii is a slightly larger-growing plant, 18 inches (45 cm) in height. This has rose-pink flowers and the bonus of leaves which are deep green above and purple beneath. This peony does best against a wall or amongst shrubs.

My relationship with *P. wittmanniana* has been one of uneasy, grudging acceptance. The mistake happened early in our association when I grew it in close proximity to *P. mlokosewitschii*. Such comparisons on first acquaintance frequently lead to misunderstandings. *P. wittmanniana* has large leaves, shiny green on the upper surface and grey below. The white, lime-tinted flowers are large with a centre of red stamens. No sooner are they open to appreciation than the petals fall, and, apart from the scarlet and black of the open seed pods, the show is over for another twelve months. Given the company of blue-flowered *Brunnera* and *Polemonium*, it is a most attractive species so long as an overlong lunchbreak does not cause the proud gardener to miss the flowering time. The species was introduced from the north west Caucasus almost 150 years ago. Plants grown from seeds show variations in height from 20 up to 36 inches (50 to 90 cm), though this could have been caused by differences in soil fertility.

Early in the present century crosses were made between *P. lactiflora* and *P. wittmanniana*; 'Avant Garde' with peach-pink flowers is the best I have seen. None of the seedlings resulting from the cross set seed, a mule-like character which effectively restricts further experiments.

The crosses between *P. mlokosewitschii* and others have created nothing of real garden worth; the offspring I have seen were lacklustre – pink and white petals reminiscent of over-bleached laundry. Crosses between *P. lactiflora* and other European species offer profitable fields of exploration. No doubt in the course of time offspring from such crosses already in existence will be available to the gardening public at large.

Extensive crossing of many species has been carried out in the United States of America over the last fifty years. Some of the hybrids are worth searching through catalogues to find – 'Constance Spry', a dark pink semi-double, 'Little Dorrit', salmon-red and compact in growth, and 'Moonrise', ivory-yellow, are three which should please and reward the diligent.

Interestingly enough, one cross between *P. mlokosewitschii* and *P. tenuifolia* produced something better than washed out laundry in 'Daystart', with a fine deep-yellow petal. This is a field of hybridisation open to anyone who grows peonies, whether amateur or professional. There is no better thrill of anticipation the garden affords than that of watching a colony of hybrid seedlings growing up to the first flush of flowers.

As a garden plant the peony makes little demand on the gardener's skill. Choose a sheltered place, particularly for the early flowering types, that is shaded from the early morning sun. This is to prevent buds caught by a late frost thawing out too quickly and being damaged. Before planting, it is well to prepare the soil thoroughly, as, given proper care, the roots should not need to be lifted for twenty years or more. Dig a dressing of rotted manure or compost into the bottom of the trench using a fork – so that the soil is loosened to a depth of 18 to 20 inches (45 to 50 cm). A dusting of complete fertiliser should be raked into the soil surface two weeks before planting. Extra phosphate encourages vigorous root development. When planted, the crown (buds) should sit just on the soil surface, no deeper than the level at which they were grown at the nursery.

Propagation of the species can be easily effected by sowing seed immediately it is ripe into a sandy compost. The containers can then stand outdoors, exposed to the frost. The only protection the seeds need is from mice who devour them avidly given the chance. Germination after winter stratification should take place the following spring.

The herbaceous hybrids can be divided just as growth starts in spring. Alternatively, lifting and division can be carried out in October. Replant straight away, so that the roots do not dry out.

Paeonia wittmanniana *'Avant Garde'*

The various forms of tree peony, *P. suffruticosa* and others, apart from being grafted as previously described, can also be layered. Before growth begins in the spring, rake a dressing of sand and peat into the soil to bed the layer into. Use shoots of the previous year's growth, and make a cut between 4 to 6 inches (10 to 15 cm) from the tip, just deep enough to form a tongue 2 inches (5 cm) long. Peg the tongued branch firmly in place, then cover with the peat and sand compost. Rooting should have taken place well enough by the following spring for the layer to be potted up.

Rumours and paintings of Chinese origin suggest that yellow, green, and dark red tree peonies were grown there hundreds of years ago. Paintings in the Lindley Library support the theory that crosses had been made then between *P. lutea*, *P. delavayi*, and *P. suffruticosa*.

With modern propagation techniques all things are possible – and who knows what new brightly-coloured hybrids will grace our gardens in the years ahead.

5 Narcissus (Daffodils)

There are some flowers which even the most determined non-gardener recognises immediately and greets with affection. Daffodils are one of the select band of universally popular plants. The name, so legend relates, derives from a handsome youth of Boeotia who, it was foretold, would live content unless and until he saw his own face. One day he stopped to slake his thirst in a pool, saw the reflection of his own beautiful features mirrored in the still water, and became so captivated he refused to be moved from the spot. Bewitched, he languished and died. Then, as Ovid relates, a flower sprang from the youth's corpse. Anyone who cares may look in the flower's cup and discover there the tears of Narcissus.

There is an interesting link between the poppy and Narcissus in the same legend. Pluto employed a flower of Narcissus to entice Ceres' daughter, Persephone, to the underworld. The poppy was created to enable the stricken Ceres to forget her grief in sleep. Other writers, less romantically inclined, say the name comes from the flower's narcotic qualities and its ability to dull the senses. That all the stories of a flower so pleasantly simple and beautiful are based on conceit or deceit is to do narcissus an unkindness. Shakespeare encompasses the character of all the lovely race in his *A Winter's Tale* – 'daffodils, That come before the swallow dares, and take The winds of March with beauty.' Poets other than Shakespeare praised the Lent lily and daffodowndilly, names which were formed from a still older title affodill, a corruption of *Asphodelus*, which now relates to an entirely different family.

Narcissi have been grown in gardens for close on four hundred years. Gerard lists a selection in his 1597 Herbal, while Parkinson in the early 1630s writes of seventy or eighty different kinds. Then for two hundred years interest in the development declined, a curious neglect which defies explanation. That the scent from the flowers was supposed to have a baneful influence causing headaches, melancholy, even insanity, may have limited the popularity of narcissi as decorative plants. This could be an exaggeration of pollen allergy; presumably there were people in those days who suffered from what is now described as hay fever, and some narcissus, par-

Narcissus pseudonarcissus captivated by its own reflection

Left: *Narcissus watieri*

ticularly the species *N. tazetta* and *N. jonquilla*, do have a very high perfume. Development of the flower in recent years more than makes up for the two centuries of neglect.

The greatest concentration of species occurring naturally is in the Mediterranean regions, Spain and Portugal being especially well endowed. Hybridisation occurs quite freely where the range of natural species overlaps, for example, *N.* × *medioluteus* (syn. *N. biflorus*) is suspected of being a natural hybrid of *N. poeticus* × *tazetta* by some authorities. Be that as it may, even without the bewildering variations in height, colour, shape, and flowering season which selective hybridisation has produced, the gardener who decides to grow species only will find these a fascinating field of exploration. From the tiny, delightful, though difficult to cultivate, *N. watieri* to the native *N. pseudonarcissus*, they welcome spring to our gardens alongside snowdrop and crocus.

Some species having been granted specific status have subsequently proved to be natural hybrids, but botanists still argue in quite heated terms on the subject. Fortunately, botanical precision is not part of the gardener's education, so when in doubt I consult the Royal Horticultural Society's Dictionary of Gardening for guidance, and then walk on tiptoe along the path the relevant page indicates.

N. asturiensis has been a garden friend and companion, tried and tested over many years. A tiny, deep yellow trumpet daffodil growing only 4 inches (10 cm) high which blooms early in the year, it is adventurously early in northern districts, and frequently suffers the punishment of weather-damaged flowers. That *N. asturiensis* grows under natural conditions some 6 to 7000 feet (1800 to 2100 m) up on mountain sides in northern Spain explains the bulbs' careless indifference to our weather. Given a sheltered corner of the rock garden which holds whatever warmth a pale February sun offers, this little species makes a lovely advance guard to the following legions.

Though all narcissus flowers share common characteristics except for modern hybrids, they do show considerable variation in size and shape of cup, as well as the petals (perianth segments in botanical terms). There is little of the obvious narcissus characteristic to be seen in the flowers of *N. bulbocodium* (hoop petticoat daffodil) to the casual eye. Certainly not in the strap-shaped, sometimes thread-like foliage, or in the curiously shaped flower. The long flaring trumpet, crinkled at the rim, and narrow petals give this variable species an elfin charm which is distinctive and attractive. There is a wide range of forms that vary from white to deep yellow. This variability occurs frequently in the wild, and this surprised me when I first saw the bulb growing under natural conditions. Native to south west France, north west Africa, Spain, and Portugal, it shows a catholic taste regarding soil type and situation. In the group I saw, some were growing in close-cropped turf near a rushing stream, others in shallow pockets of soil amongst large boulders. I suspect the rocks were limestone. There are many named varieties growing from 4 to 8 inches (10 to 20 cm) high,

Narcissus nobilis, like its near neighbour *Narcissus asturiensis*, grows wild in the mountainous regions of northern Spain

Below left:
Narcissus bulbocodium
Below:
Narcissus bulbocodium conspicuus

Right: *Narcissus* 'March Sunshine' growing with scillas

some flowering in February, others delaying until early May. However, most bloom in April. The variety *N. bulbocodium citrinus* with flowers of primrose yellow is a native of north western Spain and is deservedly popular. *N. bulbocodium conspicuus* with deep yellow flowers is a strong-growing variety, but unless divided before the bulbs get overcrowded, it produces masses of leaves only. If planted in suitable soil under grass, both of these soon spread by seed and offsets into thriving colonies. Earliest of all to flower – usually in January, and therefore best grown in a cold greenhouse, *N. bulbocodium romieuxii* is a most desirable variety with pale yellow flowers. The Spanish and north African *N. cantabricus* is now a separate species, though it is so like *N. bulbocodium* that to the non-botanist they are of the same clan. As would be expected of any bulb from that area, they need a thorough sun-baking to succeed, so they are best grown in pots – well worth the trouble just to enjoy the delicate beauty unsullied by rain.

There is no mistaking the flowers of *N. cyclamineus* with their long trumpets and curious swept-back petals. A tough little species from Spain and Portugal, if given suitable soil conditions. I find the bulbs flourish in moist yet well-drained soil, spreading self-sown seedlings to fill all the available space. When grown naturalised the height is about 8 inches (20 cm), the flower colour, a rich gold. This species is, in truth, more notable for the numerous, excellent hybrids it has sired – 'Peeping Tom', 'February Gold', 'March Sunshine' and many more supply most useful spring bulbs where space is limited.

Narcissus bulbocodium mesatlanticus

Left and above:
Narcissus cyclamineus sheltering under *Rhododendron* × *praecox*

Though the modern varieties of trumpet daffodils are a result of crosses between various species, most of the yellow forms have the subspecies *N. pseudonarcissus major* (syn. *N. hispanicus*) as a parent. Originally located in southern France and Spain, the flowers are large, golden yellow and distilling a pleasant fragrance. The height is up to 24 inches (60 cm).

N. bicolor, parent of the two-toned trumpet narcissus, has similar large flowers having a corona of golden yellow and perianth segments of white or cream. The parentage of the white trumpet daffodils is shared between three or more species. The subspecies *N. pseudonarcissus moschatus* is a small flowered and modestly drooping plant. The sulphur and white flowers open from late April to May. Grown in a mass they have an unassertive charm, more so as the flowers are delicately fragrant.

N. alpestris from the Pyrenees has the same modest demeanour, and small flowers, pure white, are borne on six inch (15 cm) stems. They open earlier than the other white species in April. Of the other stud species, *N. albescens* with off-white flowers, I know very little. It objected to the hospitality offered, for after a frugal display of blossom in two years it languished and died. Fortunately, this notable display of ill manners has not been passed on to its offspring, which in a fairly strong clay flourished exceedingly beyond all expectations. Crossing between white, yellow, and bicolor species has produced the enormous range of colours on offer at the present time. However, *N. alpestris* and *N. albescens* have been united with *N. pseudonarcissus moschatus* by modern authors – (a subspecies of great variation with a wide geographical distribution).

There is an understandable tendency to assume that all species of narcissus are hardy, adapting easily to garden conditions. While the majority do, there are some which only grow when given specialised cultivation. The jonquil, together with near relatives *N. rupicola* and *N. requienii* offer a challenge to the skill of those who attempt to grow them. The jonquil *N. jonquilla*, with rush-like leaves is one which continues to resist all my efforts. The yellow flowers carried on 10-inch (25-cm) stems are heavily perfumed. Grown in a cold greenhouse, they make a pleasant accompaniment to the alpines which also enjoy protection from inclement weather. *N. requienii*, a tiny member of the group which comes from northern Spain is a gem only 6 inches (15 cm) high. Up to five yellow flowers open on the stems, each one with a frilled central cup. Six bulbs maintain a precarious existence in the well-drained soil of a table bed. When I see the flowers which open in late March or early April being battered with heavy rain or sleet, I do feel that this fragile beauty would be happier in the greenhouse. Not so *N. rupicola*, which has made a bed half-way up a south-facing slope in the rock garden a home from home. It is hardly surprising that the bulbs thrive in stony ground, for in the wild they grow 6 to 7000 feet (1800 to 2100 m) up the mountain sides in Portugal. The flowers $1\frac{1}{2}$ inches (3.5 cm) in diameter and deep yellow in colour are carried singly on 6-inch (15-cm) stems during May. Good drainage is absolutely essential or these bulbs will not flourish. *N. juncifolius* is another fine miniature jonquil.

Spain offers another daffodil of dwarf stature which fits neatly into the small garden landscape in *N. minor*. Growing about 8 inches (20 cm) high, the flowers in two tones of yellow are large in proportion to the stem length. I grew a form with full double flowers in my last garden which came to me as 'Queen Anne's Daffodil'.

Should I ever be asked to propose an archetype daffodil, then my choice would fall on *N. pseudonarcissus* which is naturalised in so many places throughout the British Isles. There are many different forms, usually with white petals and

Top: *Narcissus jonquilla*
Above: *Narcissus juncifolius*
Below left: *Narcissus minor*
Below: *Narcissus pseudonarcissus*

lemon yellow trumpets with an average stem length of 12 inches (30 cm). The largest concentration of this species I have ever seen occurs in Farndale, Yorkshire, where the bulbs have established over many acres in the damp fields – conditions much to this daffodil's liking. The picture they make when in bloom on a sunlit April day remains vivid in the memory. At one period this species formed a convenient dumping ground for any trumpet daffodils which needed classification, including the Tenby daffodil, *N. obvallaris* with self-coloured, yellow flowers. Certainly the two are very closely related, though the Tenby daffodil lacks the robust constitution of the typical form.

There are two pheasant's eye narcissi. *N. poeticus* and the, so-called, old pheasant's eye variety, *N. poeticus recurvus* – the popular name is misleading in that the latter was introduced from Switzerland only a hundred years ago, much later than *N. poeticus*. *N. poeticus* flowers are white-petalled with a red cup, as found wild in the mountain areas of central and southern Europe. There must be many different forms, for the flowering season extended in my last garden from April until early June. *N. poeticus recurvus* has white-petalled flowers whose chrome yellow cup is edged with scarlet.

All the pheasant's eye types are scented and pleasantly so. I like to see them naturalised under apple trees in a grassed-down orchard – with the play of sunlight filtering through the branches overhead making a patina across the flowers, or growing wild, as I so frequently found them, in moist alpine meadows against the commanding landscape of the mountain above La Grave.

Of all the genus the little cup or bunch-flowered narcissus, *N. tazetta* is the most cosmopolitan. Its range extends from Syria through Kashmir to China. Paintings offer a record that this narcissus was grown in China one thousand years ago. There it is persuaded to grow in time for the Chinese new year, hence the popular name new year lily. The Tazettae section of narcissus is not easy to establish in gardens, except those with a very favourable climate, though some of the varieties bred from

Above: *Narcissus poeticus hellenicus*
Below: *Narcissus obvallaris*
Below right:
Narcissus tazetta pachybolbos

Left: *Narcissus* 'Bath Flame'
Above: *Narcissus* 'Geranium'

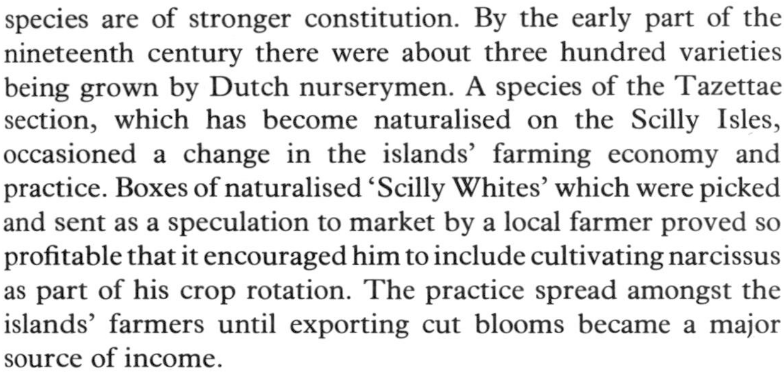

species are of stronger constitution. By the early part of the nineteenth century there were about three hundred varieties being grown by Dutch nurserymen. A species of the Tazettae section, which has become naturalised on the Scilly Isles, occasioned a change in the islands' farming economy and practice. Boxes of naturalised 'Scilly Whites' which were picked and sent as a speculation to market by a local farmer proved so profitable that it encouraged him to include cultivating narcissus as part of his crop rotation. The practice spread amongst the islands' farmers until exporting cut blooms became a major source of income.

It is a pity that the Tazettae section are not truly hardy, as the cluster-headed, sweetly-scented flowers appearing as they do so early in the year would be a most welcome addition to the garden scene. They are, however, excellent for forcing under glass; cultivated varieties such as 'Paper White' (*N. papyraceus*) and lovely 'Soleil d'Or' make a brave show in mid-winter, given just a modest amount of heat. Reports on how the narcissus was introduced to the Scillies are contradictory. The most romantic is that of a ship carrying bulbs as a cargo being wrecked on the shore – whether the bulbs were washed up on the beach or were taken ashore by looters is not clear. In fact, the suggestion that Benedictine monks carried bulbs with them from Spain when they established a cell on the island has more validity.

A cross-pollination made late in the nineteenth century by a firm of Dutch bulb growers between *N. poeticus* (pheasant's eye) and *N. tazetta* resulted in hybrids which flower later and are hardier than *N. tazetta* – known as *N.* × *poetaz*. One of the best known of the hybrids, 'Geranium' carries up to six pure white flowers per stem, each with an orange-scarlet centre.

Comparisons are easily made in some things, never between flowers do they have any great deal of meaning, yet in company with the majority of gardeners when *N. triandrus* is in flower I do feel this is, perhaps, the loveliest of all the species. As would be expected with any bulb which inhabits the north Spanish mountains, *N. triandrus albus* adapts to the cool climate of

Narcissus 'Paper White'

these islands more readily than the species from the hot sun-baked Mediterranean. In my experience the flowers last for several weeks when the bulbs are planted in shade, even seeding themselves if the bulbs are left undisturbed. I have never seen the true species except in the wild, as the bulbs sent as *N. triandrus* have always proved to be hybrids. All have greyish green rounded leaves and pendant flowers with reflexing petals. *N. triandus albus*, commonly known as the angel's tears narcissus, are white. Deep yellow-flowered forms are found in the subspecies *N. triandus concolor* and *N. triandus aurantiacus* from northern Portugal. In spite of never having acquired the true species, I find the nodding, pensive charm of *N. triandus* cultivated varieties irresistible. All of them flower during April in my garden.

I expressed the opinion previously in this chapter that *N. watieri*, a tiny jonquil, was not easy to grow and it does, in most cases, warrant that reputation. I grew six bulbs for something over ten years in a well-drained bed amongst heathers. There, this beautiful little species opened solitary, pure white flowers on 4- to 6-inch (10- to 15-cm) high stems. No doubt the heathers sucked up excess moisture, and the bulbs ripened fully as a result. Conditions identical with those which bulbs growing in the wild enjoy on steep Moroccan mountain slopes.

Narcissus triandus concolor

The choice of what species or cultivar to grow depends on the facilities the garden can offer for their accommodation. In an alpine lawn, or amongst dwarf shrubs, or ledges in the rock garden, *N. cyclamineus*, *N. minor*, *N. rupicola*, *N. bulbocodium* and cultivars derived from them will be most suitable. For naturalising, the taller *N. poeticus*, *N. pseudonarcissus*, and the stronger-growing, more vigorous hybrids are to be preferred. To provide a spring bedding, or in groups down the border, great play can be made with the brighter-petalled modern hybrids.

Narcissi thrive best in a strong, fertile, well-drained soil. They do not appreciate being planted in soil dressed with fresh farmyard manure, as I discovered to my cost some years ago. Once established, the flowering of the bulbs will be improved by an annual feed with a complete fertilizer at 2 oz (56 g) per square yard, each year in February. Bulbs are best planted in August, if possible, so that the roots are well established by the time growth stops at the onset of cold weather.

Depth of planting depends on the bulb size: smaller species 2 to 3 inches (5 to 8 cm) deep, larger-flowered species and hybrids 4 to 6 inches (10 to 15 cm) deep in bare soil, 6 to 8 inches (15 to 20 cm) deep in grassed-down land. Experiments have shown that if the foliage is left for six weeks from when the flowers fade, it can then be cut without appreciably harming the next season's blossoming. With the more temperamental species I err on the side of caution by letting the foliage wither away naturally. Narcissi are such a lovely embellishment to the spring scene that they are worth a place in the most selective gardens. That they are so widely planted is a compliment to their popularity.

6
Delphiniums

Considering that there are few plants which have contributed more to the beauty of our gardens than delphiniums, there is very little information about the origins of hybrid forms. There are upward of two hundred species, some are perennial, others biennial, while the remainder including the popular larkspur are annual. The species grow wild in North America, Europe, Asia, North Africa, and one province of China – namely Szechwan. Though three species are listed as wild plants in the British Isles, all are considered to have been introduced, even the forking larkspur, *Delphinium consolida*.

Herbalists were well acquainted with the delphinium's poisonous properties, the active principle delphinia was said to act on the nervous system. Delphinium seeds were used as a powerful purgative, as a cure for toothache, and, when mixed as a salve, to treat skin diseases. The main value of the powdered seed was its ability to destroy lice on both humans and animals, hence the popular name lousewort.

The name *Delphinium* derives from the Greek word *delphis* – a dolphin. The shape of the flower-bud, particularly that of the annual species, suggested a comparison to a leaping dolphin. Though the plants, initially, enjoyed consideration more for

Delphinium consolida

The author admiring the delphiniums at 'The Heath' near Leeds

their medicinal values than as garden decoration, for such a distinctive specimen as the delphinium there is, indeed, little more than casual reference. In the late sixteenth century note is made of a species, *D. staphisagria*, growing 2 to 3 feet (60 to 90 cm) high with flowers blue and white. This was grown, if records are correct, only in Italian gardens for medicinal purposes, and is not important in plant breeding. On the other hand *D. consolida* enjoys a somewhat better press. Once the common larkspur of gardens, this is an attractive European annual 30 inches (75 cm) high with violet or blue flowers. Records in the sixteenth century relate that it was valued as a herb for dressing wounds. Indeed, the name *consolida* – to make firm – confirms this. An infusion of the herb in water was recommended as a cure for eye complaints.

Medicinal virtues apart, the introduction of another annual, *D. ajacis*, rocket larkspur, from the Mediterranean region provided scope for the hybridist, and it is largely from this species, rather than the common larkspur, that the popular annuals so widely grown in gardens today have been developed. There is, it seems, some disagreement as to which species, *D. ajacis* or *D. consolida*, has priority – no doubt, the argument will resolve itself. Growing anything from 1 to 3 feet (30 to 90 cm) high, with double or single flowers, ranging in colour from blue, lavender, rose, pink, and white, hybrid larkspurs are easily grown in most soils as hardy annuals.

Seed is best sown directly where the plants are to flower, in April or early May. I have sown seed under cloches in September to provide early spikes of bloom for indoor decoration. Curiously, within a few years of the introduction of this species late in the sixteenth century, writers of that period were describing it as a weed in cornfields – which speaks well for adaptability if nothing else.

According to some authorities, the first truly perennial delphinium to arrive in this country was brought from the Pyrenees. Mongolia is given as the source by others. In writings on things horticultural about 1640, mention is made of both single and double forms. Described as a strong-growing perennial of up to 6 feet (1.8 m) high, with pale blue-violet flowers, *D. elatum* is considered to be the primary ancestor of popular hybrids like 'Swanlake' and 'Daily Express' grown in gardens today. Most writers on the subject agree to *D. elatum* as one parent, while suggesting by reasoned argument that the other species used in the hybridisation of delphiniums, as grown in modern gardens, are the result of work done initially by the nursery firm of Kelways which began specialist breeding of delphiniums in the mid 1800s. Fifty years or so later Blackmore and Langdon, whose name is now virtually synonymous

Right:
Delphinium 'Daily Express' with *Geranium armenum* 'Bressingham Flair' in the foreground

Prize delphiniums growing in Blackmore and Langdon's Nursery near Bristol

with delphiniums, also took an interest in the subject. American breeders, stimulated by the expressed interest from gardeners in the United States, also began experimental hybridisation, producing several fine varieties with fragrant flowers in the process.

How the smaller, repeat-flowering Belladonna hybrids like 'La Maritime' were generated is not known for certain. If looks are a guide, the neatly compact and pretty *D. grandiflorum* may lay some claim to parentage. In my experience, neither the species *D. grandiflorum*, nor the hybrids derived from it – 'Blue Bees', 'Butterfly', 'Peace', or 'Azure Fairy' are long-lived perennials, unless kept going by propagating new stock. They are, however, lovely to look at and well worth a little extra trouble even though no birth certificate is available. In certain circumstances I have sown seed of the species in April and had the resulting plants flowering in late July. There is a species closely related to *D. grandiflorum* which originates in the

Above left: *Delphinium* 'Swanlake'
Above right: An unnamed Belladonna seedling in California

Left: *Delphinium* 'La Maritime'
Right: *Delphinium* 'Blue Bees'
Far right: *Delphinium grandiflorum*

Szechwan province of China – *D. tatsienense* by name. Over the years I have grown dozens of this dwarf delphinium from seed for planting in small borders or in a rock garden. The leaves are finely divided, the violet-blue flowers with cream centre appear in mid-summer. In a sheltered, well-drained bed this species makes a good short-lived perennial. Another species suited to rock garden cultivation is *D. luteum* from California. This has attractive cream-yellow flowers and stands 12 to 18 inches (30 to 45 cm) high.

Amongst a genus with predominantly blue flowers, the appearance of two delphiniums, *D. nudicaule*, and *D. cardinale* with red-petalled blooms, is a refreshing piece of individualism. I have only grown *D. cardinale* as an annual, for the very simple reason that none of the seedlings survived the winter. It is not surprising that neither of the red-flowered species accept our climate, being natives of California. In the southern regions of that sunshine state I found *D. cardinale* growing up through poison oak on a sun-baked hillside. It grows in almost pure state, and the scenery forms a dramatic backcloth for a most

Left: *Delphinium tatsienense*
Above: *Delphinium nudicaule*

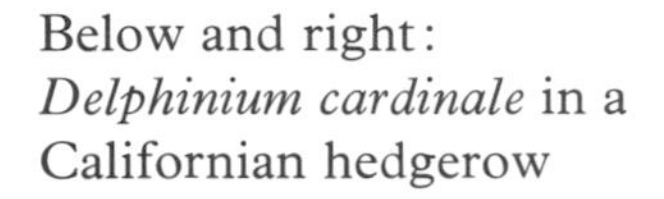

Below and right:
Delphinium cardinale in a
Californian hedgerow

Left and above:
Dr Legro's University hybrids

spectacular species. *D. nudicaule* is a pygmy, growing only 10 inches (25 cm) high with flower spikes of orange-red. The shades vary – some are better than others. Given shelter and good drainage *D. nudicaule* should be capable of surviving the winter outdoors in the maritime gardens. A hybrid between *D. nudicaule* and an unknown garden delphinium was achieved in the late 1920s after many attempts by a Dutch nurseryman. Only one seedling showed hybrid characteristics. The second generation of seedlings were of the Belladonna character with pink flowers, marketed under the cultivar name 'Pink Sensation'. In a mild climate, with good cultivation in the form of a well-prepared, freely draining soil, 'Pink Sensation' will prove a moderately sound perennial. Those, like myself, who are conditioned to mistrust our climate, will keep a stock plant indoors just in case. The height varies appreciably between 30 inches and 48 inches (0.9 and 1.2 m). It is a delightfully formed little delphinium for those who are prepared to make the effort needed to grow it successfully.

Two other species are of importance, not in their value as garden plants, but rather as tools in the hands of hybridists. *D. wellbyi* from Abyssinia with greenish-blue fragrant flowers is not sufficiently hardy to be grown outdoors. The species is being used tentatively to try and introduce a quality notably lacking in delphiniums generally – namely scented flowers. *D. zalil* from Persia is another tender importation with pale yellow flowers. Crossing between the species is not easy, requiring skill and patience, as quite often seedlings from the interpollination have proved sterile. The man who for many years has been conducting experiments in breeding delphiniums is Dr R. A. Legro, who began work in the University of Wagenin-

Delphinium 'Blue Tit'

gen in Holland thirty years ago, and has continued at the Royal Horticultural Society's garden at Wisley. He has used the species *D. zalil* with the red-flowered *D. nudicaule* and *D. cardinale*. The aim of Dr Legro was to breed hardy border delphiniums with large spikes of yellow, red, and orange flowers to complement those with the blue or white flowers normally available in commerce. To a degree this has been successful, although the limited number of the pink and fawn-coloured varieties I have tried lack the robust constitution of established *D. elatum* cultivars. Grown on strong clay soil, they showed a lessened resistance to fungal infection. Though I understand that varieties are now available which are sound perennials of robust constitution, it will be a major landmark in garden history to have delphiniums combining pink, yellow, or blue flowers with fragrance. To share the popularity of *D. elatum*, they must be adaptable to a wide range of soils, climatic conditions, and be easily increased by means of cuttings.

Work done in America during the 1950–70s resulted in the Pacific hybrid strain of delphiniums which grow from seed to flower very quickly. Under our climatic conditions they are better grown as annuals or biennials. They show a wide range of flower colour including with the normal blue and purple, shades of pink, fawn, and white. Seed sown under glass in March will provide the garden with a display of blossom during August and September which extends the delphinium's season considerably. Treated as biennials, Pacific hybrids flower in late May giving spikes of fine quality.

The even more recent strains of dwarf delphiniums which are available, and can be easily raised from seed, make a very lovely addition to the range. Those I have grown, namely 'Blue Tit' and 'Blue Jade', produced spikes of flowers 30 to 36 inches (75 to 90 cm) high. 'Blue Tit' are mostly double-flowered in indigo-blue with a small black-brown eye. 'Blue Jade' has

Delphinium 'Blue Jade'

Left: *Delphinium* 'Butterball'
Centre: *Delphinium* 'Strawberry Fair' at the Royal Horticultural Society's Garden at Wisley

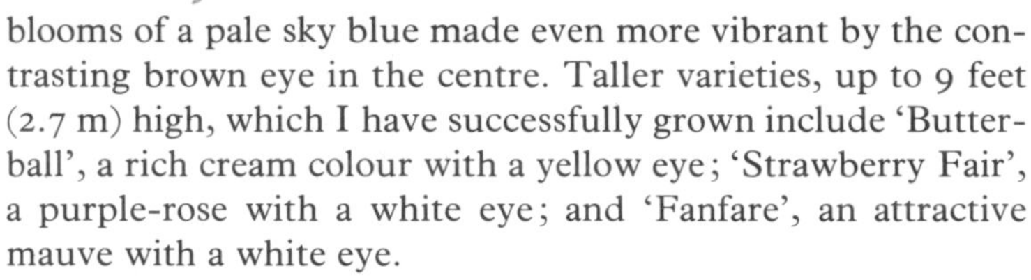

blooms of a pale sky blue made even more vibrant by the contrasting brown eye in the centre. Taller varieties, up to 9 feet (2.7 m) high, which I have successfully grown include 'Butterball', a rich cream colour with a yellow eye; 'Strawberry Fair', a purple-rose with a white eye; and 'Fanfare', an attractive mauve with a white eye.

New techniques in plant breeding will, I am sure, see an ever-increasing variation in the quality and range of delphiniums. In California new dwarf delphiniums have been bred which are only 18 inches to 3 feet (45 to 90 cm) high. All the plants I saw growing had good, well-formed flower spikes in almost every shade of blue, and recent developments have produced plants with white flower spikes. This surely must be an advantage for the smaller garden, with no need for staking being an added bonus. In general, delphiniums are not hard to grow so long as basic requirements of soil and shelter are met. They need a soil which is deep, well-drained and fertile. The plants die back to soil level, so each year they have to make an enormous amount of new growth, then yield a flower spike – a feat only possible if the roots are in a rich soil. Anyone who has lifted five-year-old delphiniums and seen the amount of root development will appreciate just how deep delving they are.

The ideal site would be in the open, exposed to all the sunshine available, yet sheltered from strong winds. To prepare the soil whether it is heavy clay, light sand, or all grades between, trench dig the bed in the autumn prior to spring planting. Though it may sound laborious, make certain this initial preparation is thorough. After opening up a 20-inch (50-cm) wide trench, lay manure, compost, or whatever organic matter is available in the bottom. Fork along the trench bottom breaking up any hard-panned soil and mix in the organic material. This should give a working depth of 20 inches (50 cm) or so, well-drained in winter yet moisture retentive in summer. Plenty of moisture is important as the delphinium makes virtu-

Right: *Delphinium* 'Fanfare'

ally all its growth in April, May and June when rainfall is spasmodic. In the late winter when the soil has settled give the bed a dressing of lime. A simple pH test will give a rough guide as to how heavy the application should be. Delphiniums, like most herbaceous plants find a neutral soil most acceptable. Lime improves the structure of clay soil, releases certain essential minerals, and neutralises acids.

Planting up the bed can be carried out towards the end of April. Delphinium species and cultivars are easily raised from seed providing it is harvested and sown quickly. Alternatively the seed can be harvested, cleaned, then stored in a cool temperature of 34 to 38°F. (1 to 3°C.) until sowing time. Delphinium seed loses viability, but cool storage conditions prevent this happening. Though the seed can be sown directly where the plants are to flower, the gardener has more control over germination if the work is done in a frame or greenhouse. Either peat- or loam-based compost can be used, but in practical terms John Innes seed compost has proved most reliable over the twenty years or more I have grown delphiniums. A high temperature is not essential for germination – 55 to 60°F. (12 to 16°C.) is quite adequate. Higher temperatures and humidity increases the risk of seedlings damping off. The seedlings of both annual and perennial species are pricked off when large enough to handle. Annuals will do well in seed boxes; perennials suffer root disturbance at planting-out time unless they are grown on in pots. Once again, the peat- or loam-based mixtures are suitable, though if seed was grown in one or the other the young plants should be kept on the same diet. My seedlings go from John Innes seed compost to the No. 1 potting mixture. Just prior to planting, about 2 weeks beforehand, dress the plot with 2 oz (56 g) per square yard of complete fertilizer.

Established plants already growing in the garden are best increased by means of basal cuttings, made from young shoots which push up from the root crowns in early spring. Some shoot-thinning on delphiniums is essential, for, if all are left to develop, the flower spikes will be of poor quality and overcrowded. Sever the cuttings close to the rootstock, then dibble them either into pots or a cold frame filled with a compost of 2 parts sharp sand and 1 part peat. Cuttings which show black marks or hollow stems are best discarded. Shoots 4 inches (10 cm) long, slightly thicker than a pencil, offer good cutting material. In my experience no extra heat is needed to help the cuttings to root – the cool and slow technique makes the sturdiest plants. Usually rooting takes place in 4–5 weeks, and the cuttings are ready for potting off into 3-inch (7-cm) pots filled with John Innes No 2. compost. Cuttings taken in early April should be ready for planting in their flowering positions by July.

Though the progressive improvement in both the quality and colour of flowers is largely a result of specialist skill assisted by modern science, anyone can make crosses which will create an interesting crop of seedlings. Usually the lower florets which open first are selected for pollination. Choose a spike to be the seed parent then, just as the flowers start to open, remove the petals (eye or bee petals) which protect the anthers and ovaries. Using a pair of tweezers remove the anthers very carefully – this emasculates the floret so preventing self-pollination. At

Above: A field in California of *Delphinium* 'Blue Springs', a dwarf variety

Delphinium 'Snowdon'

this stage the ovaries are very small and hard to see, and great care must be exercised to ensure they are not damaged. The pollen from the plant selected as the male parent is transferred to the stigma of the prepared floret immediately it is sufficiently mature. This is indicated when the tip of the stigma secretes a sticky substance, which holds the pollen grains firmly. After pollination is completed enclose the treated floret in a muslin bag to prevent unscheduled, extra pollination by insects. As the seed capsule swells it is advisable, though not essential, to strip all the other florets from the stem as the petals fade. This concentrates the plant's energy on the legitimate seed, instead of wasting it unnecessarily on capsules which are eventually going onto the compost heap.

Raising a healthy batch of young delphinium seedlings from your own selected parents and watching them coming into flower for the first time is both exciting and rewarding. But if you want to see how the experts fare, then visit the trials field in the Royal Horticultural Society's garden at Wisley where the best plants are selected and subsequently given awards. In 1983 some of the best were *D.* 'Corinth' (which received an Award of Merit), and *D.* 'Emily Hawkins' and *D.* 'Snowdon' (both gaining First Class Certificates).

Delphinium 'Emily Hawkins'

7
Dianthus and Carnations

What's in a name? A great deal when applied to some plants; and surely, Theophrastus writing in 300 BC must have been poetically inspired when choosing the name for *Dianthus*. Divine flower, blossom of Jove or Zeus, whichever translation that learned writer intended, each aptly describes a plant whose popularity continues undiminished over the passage of centuries. The genus is a large one of over three hundred species, including members which are better known by their popular names – sweet William, carnation, and pink.

So often, flowers which delighted the embryo gardener are discarded as other plants are introduced and experience ripens in maturity. Some, such as the dianthus, survive the test of time to become an essential part of the pattern. Both carnations and pinks have been cultivated in gardens for so long that the early stages of development which resulted in the flowers grown today are not recorded.

Our own native *Dianthus armeria*, the Deptford pink, which is a biennial, gives a fair indication of what the ideal conditions are for the family. Now somewhat of a rarity, it can still be found on sandy, dry pastures. So without exception, dianthus prefer a well-drained soil and a place in full sun. Even so, to maintain healthy, well-flowered specimens it is essential to keep rejuvenating them by raising fresh stock from cuttings.

Dianthus armeria

Dianthus 'Frances Isobel'

Fortunately, young growths pulled off the parent plant in late summer will root readily when inserted into a sandy compost. Seed offers an alternative method of increasing stock of the species, and can be sown immediately it is ripe, or in April at the start of the growing season. A loam- or peat-based compost will give an adequate germination, though I have a personal preference for the John Innes seed mixture when sowing pink or carnation seed.

The carnation is supposed to have obtained its name from the flesh-coloured flowers, yet early writers refer to the flowers as coronations. The name gilliflower is easier to discover, being a corruption of the Latin specific name *caryophyllus*, a clove. This is a reference to the spicy odour of the

Dianthus 'George Woodfield'

flowers which were used as a substitute for the expensive Indian cloves, much sought after as a flavouring in the preparation of certain dishes. Clove pinks were highly commended by herbalists as a treatment for nervous disorders, and to induce perspiration in those suffering from typhus and other fevers.

The carnation is derived from the species *Dianthus caryophyllus* which, according to the Royal Horticultural Society's Dictionary of Gardening, varies little in nature, though a great deal under cultivation. Several different forms do, however, occur in the Atlas Mountains, which tends to confirm Pliny's opinion expressed two thousand years ago that it is of Spanish origin. Certainly, legend has it that the carnation was brought to this country by the Normans and that the Moors were growing double carnations in the thirteenth century. It is said that it was these, when introduced to Europe from Tunis, which made them such a popular garden flower. The species *D. caryophyllus* has a deep-pink flower, so other species must have been used to procure the many and various shades available at the present time. Possibly *D. knappii* with a nondescript yellow flower may have played a part. In the sixteenth century double dianthus were illustrated in Persian pottery and tiles. The petals of these early hybrids usually show stripes or splashes of a different colour tone. Variously known as picotees and bizarres, it is not recorded whether they resulted from contrived cross-pollination or as a result of selection from random crosses.

In the middle of the eighteenth century a repeat blooming

Dianthus 'Fragrant Ann'

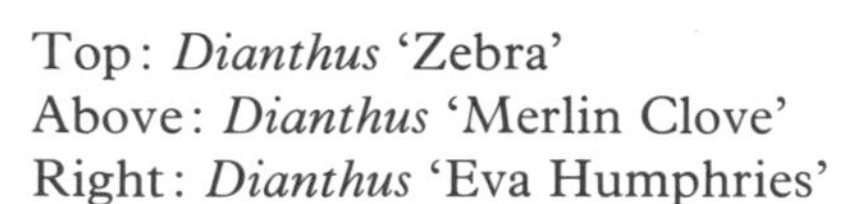

Top: *Dianthus* 'Zebra'
Above: *Dianthus* 'Merlin Clove'
Right: *Dianthus* 'Eva Humphries'

carnation, which flowered from June until September, was raised in southern France. At about the same time carnations were being suggested more as a pot plant for the greenhouse than as a perennial to be grown in the open garden. The nineteenth century saw the introduction of perpetual 'Malmaison' and 'Chabauds' strains. Even under glass and with the modern aids to cultivation enjoyed today, it takes skill to grow perpetual and Malmaison carnations well. How the perpetual carnation was achieved is not known for certain. One suggestion which seems the most credible is that it is a hybrid between *D. caryophyllus* and the Chinese or Indian pink, *D. chinensis*, an annual or sometimes biennial species with pink or white flowers flecked and spotted with dark red. So once again it is a union between east and west which, as with roses, has been responsible for introducing a popular perennial to garden cultivation.

The breeding of perpetual carnations was for many years confined to France and America. 'Mrs Thomas W. Lawson', a cerise-pink, and 'Victor Emmanuel', crimson and scarlet on yellow, were two important stud varieties – parents of a whole new generation of florists' perpetual carnations. The British contribution, with cultivars 'Winter Cheer' crossed earlier this century with 'Mrs Thomas W. Lawson', gave 'Brittania' – a delightful non-fading scarlet-flowered form. Nowadays, varieties such as 'Fragrant Ann', white, 'George Woodfield', cream, edged with crimson, and 'Joanne', deep cerise, are among the showmen's favourites.

As the parent of border and perpetual carnations with their brightly coloured, sweetly-scented flowers, *D. caryophyllus* is a classic example of floral development at the hands of gardener hybridists.

Border carnations should be planted in a sunny position into a soil which is well drained. Prepare the site by digging in a light dressing of well-rotted compost or farmyard manure, burying it about 8 to 10 inches (20 to 25 cm) deep. On heavier soil a bed raised about 6 inches (15 cm) above the general level will make sure of good drainage, essential if the plants are to thrive. The young stock is planted 15 to 18 inches (38 to 45 cm) apart in April. Reliable varieties include 'Eva Humphries' – white ground picotee with dark red edging, 'Merlin Clove' – white, marked with crimson, 'Zebra' – yellow, marked with crimson, and 'Harmony' – grey-flecked cerise.

Annual carnations require similar soil conditions and spacing. Most varieties will grow between 2 to 3 feet (60 to 90 cm) high, so some form of support is necessary. The carnation hoops made from heavy gauge galvanised wire serve the purpose best, and are inconspicuous as well. To ensure good quality blooms, as the flower stems develop remove all buds except those at the tips of the shoots. A feed of bone meal or similar organic fertiliser applied each year in spring will maintain the soil fertility. 'Fire Carpet', Chabaud and 'Queens Court' are recommended strains.

The cultivation of perpetual flowering carnations in a greenhouse is both interesting and rewarding. Given good light in a well-ventilated atmosphere, with a winter temperature of 45–50°F. (7–10°C.) minimum the carnation will produce good crops of flowers. The young cuttings should be grown in John Innes No 1 compost in a pot no larger than 3½ inches (9 cm) to begin with. When large enough, transfer to 6 inch (15 cm) pots

Below left: *Dianthus* 'Queens Court'
Below: *Dianthus* 'Vera Woodfield'

Dianthus plumarius

Dianthus 'Sussex Fortune'

filled with John Innes No 2 compost. Pinch out the growing tip when ten pairs of leaves have formed. This will encourage side shoots to grow, and these should be stopped at five leaves. How many more stops are made depends on when the plants are required to flower – two stops will mean an autumn crop. As the flower buds develop give a feed – either dry or liquid at ten day intervals. Remove all buds except the crown bud at the top. Top show varieties include 'Sussex Fortune' – brilliant scarlet, striped crimson, 'Boltonian' – crimson, and 'Vera Woodfield' – pale yellow.

Cuttings made from non-flowering side shoots, taken in winter and inserted in sharp sand over bottom heat, will root in four to six weeks. Seed is an alternative method of propagation, and often creates interesting colour forms. It can be sown into pots filled with seed compost in February to March.

Garden pinks enjoy a wider acclaim than the carnation, possibly because they need less specialised cultivation. Though several species are thought to have contributed, the main parent is *D. plumarius* which grows in lime-rich soil and in the mountainous terrain of south-western Europe. The fragrant, fringe-petalled flowers on 4- to 12-inch (10- to 30-cm) high stems are pink. In natural conditions, forms with white and deeper pink flowers with a central blotch have been recorded. These offered early hybridists material to work with and select from.

Our own native Cheddar pink, *D. gratianopolitanus*, also with fringed pink-petalled flowers is one species almost

Top left: *Dianthus* 'Diane'
Below left: *Dianthus* 'Mrs Sinkins'

Top: *Dianthus* 'Laced Monarch'
Centre: *Dianthus* 'Doris'
Below: *Dianthus* 'Ruby Doris'

certainly used for cross-pollination with *D. plumarius*. Laced pinks which were a favourite of the Paisley weavers own the same ancestry as the well-known *D.* × *allwoodii* and were obtained by crossing border carnations with established varieties of garden pink. So in reality, though *D. plumarius* is the prime progenitor, the Cheddar pink, Chinese pink, and carnation all assisted at one stage or another in creating the garden pink.

The hybrids are grouped in colours as selfs or single coloured; bicolours – with two distinct shades; laced – where the petals are edged with the same shade as that of the central blotch; and fancies where the petals are flecked with irregular markings.

Garden pinks grow from 10 to 15 inches (25 to 38 cm) high and have grey-green leaves with single or double flowers, usually appearing in June to July. Good old varieties include 'Mrs Sinkins' – white petalled and very fragrant, 'Inchmery' – pale pink, and 'Excelsior' – carmine with a darker central eye.

A well-drained soil which contains lime is suitable for the majority of garden pinks. I find that digging the site over, incorporating just a sprinkling of compost or well-rotted manure in the autumn before planting up-rooted cuttings in the spring, works very well. To help the young plants establish and form side shoots, I nip out the growing point six weeks after planting. A dressing of peat and bone-meal fertiliser plus a dusting of sulphate of potash lightly raked into the soil in March each year helps maintain vigour and flower yield. Cuttings of non-flowering side shoots taken in June to July root in four to six weeks if dibbled into a sandy compost.

Of the modern varieties, 'Doris' with salmon pink flowers, and a sport 'Ruby Doris' are my favourites. Other varieties which have done very well for me include 'Prudence' – pale pink with a darker centre, 'Freckles' – pink flecked red, and 'Diane', salmon pink.

That within a single genus there are so many markedly different races of notable garden plants of ancient lineage is remarkable. For *D. barbatus* – the sweet William – is an old-established favourite which grows wild in southern Europe. In 1535 they were being sold at 3d per bushel, so even at that time they must have been well-known garden plants. To judge from the illustration I have seen, though sweet William have been cultivated for a long time, there has been no dramatic change in the shape or size of the flowers. Annual sweet William are available which flower during July from seed sown under glass in February which is a fairly modern innovation. They grow 6 inches (15 cm) high with flowers a replica in miniature of the more widely grown biennial forms. Sweet William of tradition are usually treated as biennials. The seed is sown in a prepared bed in May, and the seedlings are then large enough for transplanting to their flowering positions in September.

A cross made between sweet William and a garden pink (*D.* × *allwoodii*) produced a larger, more colourful strain which is marketed under the name 'Sweet Wivelsfield'. All will succeed in good garden soil to which lime has been added, and

Top left: *Dianthus seguieri*
Below left: *Dianthus gratianopolitanus*

they flower at their lovely best when given a place in full sun. Seed strains of sweet William are also available which will display flowers all of the same colour, a great advantage when planning colour schemes to give the best effect in the garden.

There are species other than those already mentioned as parents of carnations, garden pinks, and sweet William which are well worth a place in rock garden or herbaceous border. They have the advantage of breeding true when raised from seed, and this offers an easy, inexpensive way of adding choice plants to the collection.

D. alpinus from the Austrian Alps forms a hummock of green foliage and blossoms over several weeks from June to August. Individual flowers are large in proportion to the overall size of the cushion, and the colour varies from pink to light purple with a contrasting paler centre. The height of 4 to 6 inches (10 to 15 cm) makes it suitable for growing in the smaller

Dianthus 'Spencer Bickham'

rock garden. Another species that is a very suitable rockplant is *D. seguieri*, which has its home in northern Spain. Other varieties of dianthus which make attractive alpines are 'Spencer Bickham' – with a profusion of pink flowers, and 'Garland' – a good ground cover with pure pink flowers.

D. gratianopolitanus, the Cheddar pink mentioned previously as one parent of the ubiquitous garden pink, is well worth growing on its own merit. When the carpet of glaucous grey-green foliage is embroidered with the fragrant pink flowers during the summer, few plants are more pleasing. A variety known as 'La Bourbrille' is a mirror image of the parent in dwarf form, and it is not too large for a trough garden or table bed. I have had Cheddar pinks in various forms still flowering like young plants after ten years or more.

Though the species *D. chinensis* is not commonly listed in seed catalogues, named varieties derived from it are obtainable.

Of these, 'Heddewigii' shows the intricate markings on the petals which is such a characteristic of the species. 'Fireball' is a useful, double scarlet-flowered form, while 'Baby Doll' with mixed coloured blooms on 6-inch (15-cm) stems offers a prospect for the small garden or window box.

One of the most adaptable dianthus I have grown to date is the maiden pink, *D. deltoides*. The name puzzles me, for there is little I can discover about the plant which suggests the triangle the name implies, unless it is the way each flower-stem divides. I found no problems in my last garden on heavy clay in keeping *D. deltoides* happy, and on the lighter soil in this area of Yorkshire the colonies maintain themselves by self-sown seedlings – a commendable piece of private enterprise. A native of Europe including Great Britain, according to some sources, the height varies depending on location, from between 6 and 12 inches (15 and 30 cm). The narrow leaves are dark green, and the flowers in the best forms are red through to pink. Varieties of *D. deltoides* which offer colour variation are 'Brilliant' – rose,

Above: *Dianthus* 'Alice'

Below: *Dianthus deltoides*

'Queen of Hearts' – scarlet, and my own choice formed from long acquaintance 'Erectus' – in a glowing, vivid red.

D. pavonius (syn. *D. neglectus*) is curious in my own observation in that it seems happier growing on acid soil rather than one containing lime. To see the short-cropped turf on the alpine pastures near La Grave, pink and red-shaded with the myriad flowers of this lovely dianthus made me desire it for my own rock garden. They make dense tufts of greyish green leaves and in summer large, deep crimson flowers an inch (2.5 cm) or more across, if careful selection is made of plants grown from seed. One characteristic common to all is that the back of each petal is coloured bronze. There are few species more worth raising from seed than this, so that selection can be made of the best colour variations. These can then be propagated by means of cuttings taken in early summer.

In all the books I have read on the subject of dianthus there is one name, that of Montague Allwood, which occurs more frequently than any other, indeed, to British gardeners the pink and Allwood are virtually synonymous. The results of his labours are recorded by the attribution *allwoodii*, but his legacy to gardens extends much further. By introducing the *allwoodii* stock into the breeding lines, a whole new race of perpetual flowering pinks has been established. The first *allwoodii* hybrids were the progeny resulting from a cross between *D. plumarius* and the perpetual flowering carnation. 'Alice', 'Daphne', 'Paul', 'Thomas', and numerous others are a living memorial to his skill as a hybridiser.

In seeking to expand the boundaries of exploration he then crossed *D.* × *allwoodii* hybrids with dwarf alpine species such as *D. alpinus*, *D. gratianopolitanus* and others to give *D.* × *allwoodii* 'Alpinus'. This gave plants of dwarf habit with attractive grey foliage and sweetly-scented flowers in a wide range of colours. 'Prince Charming', 'Goblin', 'Little Jock', and 'Fay' all derive in some way from Mr Allwood's first explorations. Many of the modern Show pinks owe parentage, possibly some distance removed to the Allwoodii line.

Dianthus 'Daphne'

In addition to the crosses between sweet William (*D. barbatus*) and *D.* × *allwoodii*, re-crosses were made between the offspring which resulted and other dianthus species. 'Sweet Wivelsfield', 'Delight', and the 'Loveliness' strain with heavily fringed petals combine the best qualities of their parents, plus hybrid vigour which makes them excellent bedding plants. All of them are available in seed form. This offers the easiest method of raising a generous stock for bedding work.

With so many species and garden varieties to work among, dianthus presents a profitable field of exploration to the amateur who wishes to discover some of the excitement and fascination of raising new varieties. At the most it only means a waiting period of two years before the offspring of a cross-pollination between dianthus flowers. Those who do decide to step into the shoes of yesterday's plant breeders should always keep a record of any crosses made. After all, even a dianthus of supreme quality requires a pedigree before it can be registered.

8
Pelargoniums and Geraniums

Geraniums and pelargoniums are so closely akin that at one period in botanical history they were all grouped in one genus. Though the process of cross-pollination to produce new forms of pelargonium has to some extent masked the distinguishing features, they are still revealed by close examination.

The name geranium is derived from the Greek *geranos*, a crane. The members of the genus have regular flowers, the petals of equal size, and the seed pod, as the common name implies, straight – shaped like a crane's-bill. Most are hardy when grown outdoors in the British Isles, being natives of the Northern Hemisphere. All the pelargonium species have irregularly shaped flowers, with two upper petals frequently overlapping and three, often smaller, lower petals. Usually the flowers are spurred, and the seed capsule beaked, splitting into spiral segments when ripe. In spite of the genera having been separate for well over a hundred years, the usual common name for *Pelargonium* is still geranium.

Native to South Africa, Madagascar, Arabia, and similar regions favoured with a warmer climate than our own, it is not surprising that pelargonium species and cultivars are tender, and need heated greenhouse protection in winter if they are to survive. The name is derived from *pelargos* – a stork – the shape of the fruit bearing a fancied resemblance to the bird's beak.

Pelargonium is a large and complicated genus, as anyone who tries to disentangle the species will discover. The confusion was compounded by some botanists in the nineteenth century refusing to accept the division of *Pelargonium* and *Geranium* into separate genera. When the threads of history are sorted out it is the parentage of the regal pelargonium which is the most complex. 'Fringed Aztec', 'Hazel Cherry' and 'Honeywood Lindley' are typical of this group. *Pelargonium* × *domesticum*, the regal, is derived from crosses between possibly eight species, though I have consulted no authority able to be precise on this point. Of these species, four are especially important. *P. angulosum*, a shrubby species about 3 feet (90 cm) high introduced in the first quarter of the eighteenth century, has purple-carmine flowers which open during the three months August to October. *P. cucullatum*, which arrived about twenty-five years

Above: *Pelargonium cucullatum*, ancester of the Regal strains, on the Cape Peninsula

Left:
Pelargonium 'Hazel Cherry' (Regal)
Right:
Pelargonium 'Fringed Aztec' (Regal)

Pelargonium peltatum growing up through a thornbush on a sunbaked hillside in South Africa

before *P. angulosum*, has the same habit, albeit having greater vigour, and the flowers are crimson with deeper veins. The shape and habit is the dominant character contributed by these two. One of the first species to arrive was *P. triste*, brought by one John Tradescant in 1632.

Two species, *P. fulgidum* with petals of bright, fiery red, and *P. grandiflorum*, dwarfer in stature with white flowers, added positively to the wide colour range now seen in the hybrids. Other species which arrived at this time were *P. graveolens* and *P. radens*.

There was promiscuous crossing between the species in the early nineteenth century, and, as with other popular garden plants, hybrid was crossed with hybrid, then back-crossed, until it is a wise pelargonium which knows its own mother, let alone the male parent. Few records were kept of the crosses, so exact pedigrees will never be discovered. But one early hybrid was *P. tricolor*, and it survives today.

P. peltatum, the ivy-leaved geranium, was introduced some time about the year 1700, and has not been subject to the same frenetic intercrossing. Though crosses have been made, these

Below left:
Pelargonium fulgidum flowering in South African scrubland
Below:
Pelargonium 'Duke of Edinburgh' (Ivy-leaved)

Pelargonium tricolor on a stony scree in its native home

have influenced flower colour rather than leaf shape or habit. Modern varieties which are reliable are 'Duke of Edinburgh' and 'L'Elégante'.

The third group, the zonal pelargoniums, *P.* × *hortorum*, are to most laymen just geraniums or plants with orange-scarlet flowers used by parks departments for summer bedding. Typical varieties of this group are 'Irene', 'Ashfield Monarch' and 'Elizabeth Iris'. The characteristic of this section is the horseshoe mark on the leaf. *P. zonale*, which arrived in the early 1700s, was followed shortly afterwards by the most striking of all the species, *P. inquinans* with brilliant scarlet-coloured, broad-petalled flowers. Crosses between the two species made *Geranium africanum*, as it was then called, a much admired garden flower. Strangely enough the species, *P. zonale*, in spite of the specific name, has not a heavily zoned leaf. More recently other species including the shrubby *P. acetosum*, with long narrow, strap-like rose-coloured petals have been used for cross-pollination to give an even wider range of flower colour and shape.

About one hundred years ago saw the beginning of the

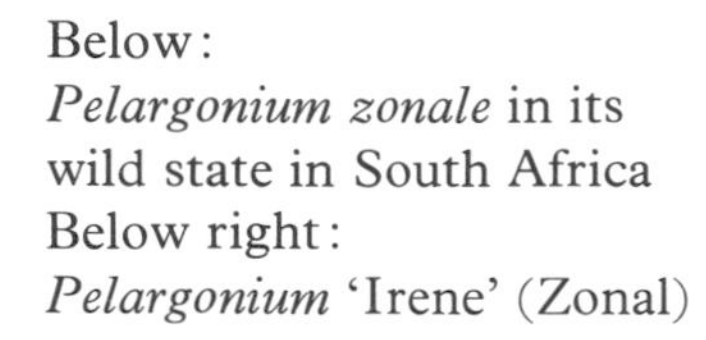

Below:
Pelargonium zonale in its wild state in South Africa
Below right:
Pelargonium 'Irene' (Zonal)

Pelargonium 'Picasso'

golden age of pelargoniums, when gardeners in private service and local parks began to propagate the zonal or nosegay geraniums for use in massed bedding schemes. The first double was raised in France by the nursery of Lemoine which seems to have specialised in creative hybridisation. Just eighty years ago 'Paul Crampel', the most famous of all pelargoniums, was put on the market. I doubt very much if at the present time any plant has been more widely used for summer bedding. This vivid scarlet pelargonium together with the blue lobelia and the white alyssum brings summer to city gardens throughout the British Isles.

With the advent of the modern F1 hybrid cultivars of pelargonium, unbelievably still listed as geraniums in seed catalogues, a new era has opened. Seed sown under glass in January or February will give flowering-size plants for bedding out during early June, this doing away with the more laborious, time-consuming routine of raising thousands of plants from cuttings each year. For specially effective bedding schemes varieties can be bought which, even when raised from seed, will give flowers all of one colour. 'Mustang', brilliant scarlet, 'Picasso', purplish carmine, and 'Sundance', orange-scarlet, are some of the newcomers which have revolutionised pelargonium cultivation. The dwarf varieties like 'Video' and 'Playboy' are useful for tubs, window boxes, or gardens where there is limited space. The F1 hybrid 'Orange Cascade' has a trailing pendulous growth which is best displayed in hanging baskets or similar positions where a cascade of bloom can be used to good effect. The leaves carry the characteristic zoned markings. However, the zonal pelargoniums offer more than attractively flowered varieties, for there are some available with leaves that are prettily coloured also. The foliage forms (fancy-leaved) are not

Pelargonium capitatum on the Cape Peninsula

Pelargonium 'Tuesday's Child'

by any means a modern innovation, for mention is made of painted leaf, or striped, crane's-bills over two hundred years ago. An old hybrid is 'Miss Burdett Coutts', and a more modern variety, 'Tuesday's Child'.

Mr Peter Grieve, a gardener who lived in Bury St Edmunds about 1850, was the first person to take a practical interest in the breeding of variegated or fancy-leaved pelargoniums. In common with most variegated plants, the fancy-leaved varieties require a little more care to grow than those with plain green leaves. Some are bi-coloured with silver or gold banding, others are tri-coloured with red, purple, and other shades added, while 'Red Black Vesuvius', a miniature, has foliage so dark as to be almost black with only a trace of green showing.

The scented-leaved pelargonium became a most popular pot plant, enjoying lodgings in baronial hall and cottage window sill with admirable impartiality. The foliage is so strongly perfumed that just brushing the leaves brings out the distillation. Many are species, others are hybrids principally derived from two species, *P. crispum* and *P. graveolens*. *P. crispum* is an erect-branching shrub, growing 3 feet (90 cm) or more in height, and having a strong citrus scent to its foliage. The cultivar 'Variegatum', with cream and white marbled foliage, is commonly grown. *P. graveolens* hybrids with more deeply divided leaves are known as rose-scented pelargoniums. Another fragrant plant is *P. ×fragrans*, smelling of nutmeg, and believed now to be hybrid (*P. exstipulatum* × *P. odoratissimum*).

Other species with rose-scented leaves include *P. capitatum* with deeply cut leaves and small rose and purple flowers, also *P. denticulatum* with the most fern-like foliage of all. Indeed, so fern-like is the appearance that the tiny whitish flowers come as something of a surprise.

Propagation of all pelargoniums is by seed sown either in January or February in a temperature maintained at about 65°F. (18°C.). Either peat- or loam-based composts are suitable, and the seedlings are transferred to pots when large enough to handle. Cuttings are the means of increase adopted for named varieties. These are made from young growths of 2–3 inches (5 to 8 cm), which can be taken at any time from July to September, and rooted in sandy compost before being potted into John Innes or peat-based compost.

The true *Geranium* is a genus which contains about four hundred species – most of them hardy herbaceous perennials. Most are easily grown decorative plants which will succeed in any reasonable soil. Like so many native plants, crane's-bills blend into the garden landscape, achieving an agreeable harmony which is not always possible with the aggressively coloured pelargonium. That geraniums have been cultivated in our gardens for centuries is faithfully recorded by authors writing in the sixteenth century. Both Gerard and Parkinson list four species as growing in gardens. Gardeners of the time had a poetic knack of choosing pretty, descriptive names for their plants. Who, I wonder, first called *Geranium striatum* 'Queen Anne's Needlework'? The flowers of *G. pratense* were used in Ireland for dyeing wool. On the continent geranium root is mentioned as being used to tan leather, but apart from these two uses, the family figures little in folk lore, though it is occasionally mentioned as a cure for piles and dysentry.

Geraniums vary widely in stature and flower colour over the four hundred species. Some are best accommodated in the rock garden, others are suitable for inclusion in the herbaceous border, while there are some which thrive best in the partially shaded conditions of a shrub border.

G. argenteum, whose leaves are covered in a cobweb of silvered hairs, is one of those lovely plants which, unlike the majority of the clan, is not easy to grow. The flowers are pink but there are selected forms. One I grew called 'Purpureum' had flowers deepening to royal red. The overall height is 6 inches (15 cm), and it grows best in very well-drained soil with full exposure to sunlight. A choice little rock plant well worth persisting with.

Introduced from the Pyrenees in the early 1800s *G. endressii* is altogether more robust and very pretty, a near evergreen which flowers over several months. The form 'Wargrave Pink' has the brightest salmon pink flowers and grows upwards of 18 inches (4 cm) in height. 'Winscomb' has pale mauve flowers.

Also from the Pyrenees, *G. cinereum* is more a plant for the dwarf border or rock garden. A neat hummock of rounded, grey green leaves only 6 inches (15 cm) high with large cupped flowers of pink with darker lines along the veins. The best-known form is *G.c. subcaulescens*, a compact mat of greenery with flowers of rich crimson, each centred with a darker eye. It is a plant which will enjoy being allowed comfortable elbow room along the front of a herbaceous border. A hybrid of this species, 'Ballerina', is exceptional. Its lilac-pink flowers veined

Top:
Pelargonium crispum 'Variegatum'
Above:
Geranium endressii 'Wargrave Pink'

Above and right:
Geranium 'Ballerina'
Below:
Geranium cinereum subcaulescens

with purple open in succession throughout the summer into autumn.

A small species from Albania and Yugoslavia called *G. dalmaticum* offers a different foliage character. The glossy leaves are hard-textured, taking on bright tints before withering in autumn. Flowers in a pleasant shade of pink are carried on 4-inch (10-cm) stems, and all turn neatly outwards to show full face for our appreciation. My plants grow quite happily amongst dwarf shrubs.

Geranium maderense

So many lovely plants have come from China to grace our gardens that it comes as no surprise to find a choice geranium amongst them. The botanists now insist in the name *G. napuligerum* for this species from the mountains of Kansu in China, but to me it will always be identified by the older, more illustrious name of *G. farreri*. Planted in a free-draining gritty soil, the tufts of grey-green leaves are smothered during early summer with flowers of softest pink, each with contrasting black anthers. The stems are spreading, the overall height about 6 inches (15 cm).

Though I grow *G. ibericum*, this south eastern European is outfaced to such an extent by a hybrid between it and *G. platypetalum*, that where space is limited I would choose this one, by name *G.* × *magnificum*. The leaves are deeply divided, turning yellow and pale orange at the onset of autumn. The violet-blue flowers are borne on 24-inch (60-cm) high stems during early summer.

My fondness for *G. macrorrhizum* has not diminished in over twenty years of close acquaintance. Brought from southern Europe over four hundred years ago, this 18-inch (45-cm) high crane's-bill spreads out to make a near weedproof ground cover. It is partially evergreen, but the older leaves die to produce good

Geranium × *magnificum*

Geranium macrorrhizum on the steep slopes of Mount Olympus

autumn colour. The best form, called 'Ingwersen's Variety', has flowers of rose-pink, whereas those of the type are magenta. The rounded, light green leaves are pleasantly aromatic to me, but a friend when visiting the garden described the odour in derogatory terms as similar to that of a mangy cat. This is contradicted by the fact that this species is a source for the distillation of geranium oil. It is an easily grown species which is at home in most garden soils. An attractive tender species is *G. maderense* from Madeira, with purple flowers.

G. phaeum is a western European which is well enough suited to have escaped from the confines of gardens to become naturalised. The popular name mourning widow describes the nodding, reflexed, dark purple flowers to a nicety. The species' main virtue is that it will make a pleasant light green under-cover in quite dense shade. In the open, it grows 18 inches (45 cm) high, whereas under shade it tops 24 inches (60 cm).

Native plants which are also beautiful earn a special place in gardens providing they behave in a respectable, non-invasive manner. Lovely though the violet blue flowers of *G. pratense* look in a country landscape, they make themselves too much at home in the garden by seeding all over the borders. Few have space or, indeed, the tolerance to accommodate a 3-foot (90-cm) high crane's-bill which only blooms for three weeks. The best garden form of the wild crane's-bill is 'Mrs Kendall Clarke' which flowers throughout June and July.

Geranium pratense
'Mrs Kendall Clarke'

One of the tallest species I grow at 4 feet (1.2 m) high comes from Armenia, and is identified by the name *G. psilostemon.* Introduced about a hundred years ago, it makes a boskage of elegant, deeply divided leaves, which colour well in the autumn. Succeeding in sun or partial shade, it has vivid magenta crimson, black-centred flowers during the summer.

Plants with attractive foliage afford interest extending way beyond the term granted to the flowers, and *G. renardii* is lovely in leaf, with the white-veined flowers a short term accoutrement. During the whole season sage-green leaves make a 1-foot (30-cm) high dome to complement the more extravagant colours associated with them.

Another geranium which has travelled the years of gardening with me is *G. sanguineum.* The bloody crane's-bill is one of the indispensables – a tough 12-inch (30-cm) high perennial which forms a mat of twiggy stems 18 inches (45 cm) across. The flowers which can be deep magenta through varying shades to mallow pink are a conspicuous feature from early summer. It is one of those trouble-free garden plants, easily propagated simply by pulling away pieces of the sprawling stems with roots attached. A form of this species, *G. sanguineum lancastriense* can be found growing wild on Walney Island off the coast of Lancashire, and has shell-pink flowers pencilled with crimson. I once spent a day on Walney noting all the variations in flower colour amongst the plants growing there. After identifying at least fourteen shades I decided that there is no type colour for this geranium, excellent though it is.

A notable hybrid, good as an edging plant for a wall, is 'Russell Prichard', with crimson-red flowers.

There are some weeds which, even when discovered invading those parts of the garden reserved for choice treasures, do not suffer a summary expulsion. Though a weed and an annual, herb robert, *G. robertianum,* with fern-like foliage and tiny pink flowers, can never be a nuisance. I grow it in amongst the stones which support a bank planted with native flowers, harebells, primroses, and the like.

Wood crane's-bill, *G. sylvaticum,* is described as the northern counterpart of meadow crane's-bill, with me it flowers early when the violet, white-eyed blooms are especially welcome. The leaves are rounded, deeply divided into seven lobes and are a useful weed suppressor. There are pink and white forms to be had for those who search diligently for them.

That a species from the Himalaya should prove a disappointment is sad but, in my experience with *G. wallichianum,* unfortunately true. The flowers are bluish-violet with a white eye, and are so nondescript as not to be worth a place. A seedling which appeared self-sown in the garden in Wales owned by Mr E. C. Buxton more than compensates for the parent's lack of charm. For 'Buxton's Variety' is a thoroughbred, spreading out leafy stems for 18 inches (45 cm) or more, and bearing crop after crop of large saucer-shaped white-centred blue flowers. A lightly shaded corner of the garden preserves the nemophila blue of the flowers.

Geranium sanguineum 'Holden Variety'

Above and below:
Geranium sanguineum lancastriense
at Bressingham Gardens

The species of *Geranium* are not difficult to raise from seed sown into either loam or peat-based composts. Division of the mat-formers also gives the cultivator of geraniums a method of increasing stock. In addition, all those species and varieties I grow will root from cuttings taken in summer.

Amongst my favourite varieties of a much under-rated flower, are:

G. 'Ballerina', an alpine which has dark red veins on each lilac-pink flower.

G. cinereum subcaulescens, an alpine with crimson flowers which last for many weeks.

G. pratense 'Johnson's Blue', which is about 18 inches (45 cm) high, and has attractive light-blue flowers produced in late June, early July.

9
Poppies

There are a great many flowers described in popular terminology as poppies. It is fortunate that botanists demand a more exact definition, or identifying a plant would be very difficult. To the botanist, poppies are those seventy or so species of annual or perennial plants included under the ancient Latin name of *Papaver*. The species are found growing naturally in Europe, northern Africa, western Asia to India. There are two species whose distribution is hard to fit into the general pattern: *Papaver aculeatum*, which occurs in Africa and Australia (a considerable geographical gap), and the other, *P. californicum*, a dainty little annual which to me looks like first cousin to our field poppy, and grows in the United States of America.

Geographical riddles become elementary when confronted with the wealth of myth, lyric, and legend which has grown up to disguise the historical facts of the poppy's evolution in gardening terms. That truth and fiction should be so entwined is not surprising, for the poppy in various forms has been in cultivation for upwards of 2500 years. Controversy begins immediately over the name for the genus *Papaver*. One suggestion, that it derives from the sound made when chewing the seed, suggests a vulgar gluttony, which even a personal experiment in private failed to confirm. The recording of seeds being chewed by no stretch of the imagination suggested *Papaver*, or any other word for that matter. I find Flora Medica offers a more acceptable derivation – linking the name with a Celtic word Papa or pap – the soft baby food in which poppy seeds were mixed to encourage infant slumber.

According to the ancient Greeks the poppy was created by the God of sleep to help Ceres, who was overcome by despair at being unable to recover her daughter abducted by Pluto. Ceres, unable to sleep, was neglecting her duties as the Goddess of crops. After her refreshing, poppy-induced slumber, the corn grew full to harvest. This probably, in some way, explains why *P. rhoeas* – the field poppy or corn rose – was in medieval times considered not to be a weed, but essential in corn fields for the prosperity of the crop. In more recent times, when the field of Waterloo was ploughed after Wellington's victory, the red

Papaver rhoeas growing on the coast of Crete

A Shirley poppy

poppies which grew from the newly turned soil were believed to be stained with the blood of soldiers killed in the battle. Thus the superstitions and beliefs contradictorily invest in the same flower symbolic remembrance and the fantasy of grief assuaging sleep. While from Roman times poppies have been offered as memorials to the dead, the Greeks used the flower as proof of sincere love. Young lovers placed a red petal on the palm of one hand, then struck it with the other. Should the petal snap audibly, this proved fidelity, if it failed to break, unfaithfulness. Add the fateful power of prophecy to remembrance and the gift of sleep, and the poppy gains a notable place in garden history. No plant achieves distinction unless it has merit either in economic terms, or as a beautiful addition to the garden – poppies qualify in both these spheres.

Most of the species are hardy, growing successfully in any soils providing the drainage is good, though they give of their lovely best in light, sandy loam, and a place in full sun. Propagation is easy: annual species are grown from seed which is produced in huge quantities. The perennial forms are increased by division of established plants, or in some cases, by root cuttings made in the dormant season. The larger growing perennial species are best accommodated in the mixed or herbaceous border, the annuals which are short term residents can be used to supply bright colour wherever it is needed.

The best known of all poppies, *P. rhoeas*, is familiar to gardeners and non-gardeners because it is found growing wild in fields and odd corners around the countryside. Until recently, one of the prettiest pictures July offered was that of cornfields aflame with scarlet poppies. Modern science, in the shape of selective weed controls, has virtually eliminated the poppy from everywhere except the hedgerows and waste places.

So many of our popular garden flowers owe their success to the single-minded devotion of one person. The stimulus which initially captures their interest varies. With some the love of a

Papaver somniferum 'Pink Chiffon'

particular plant, with others an observation of variation in form or flower colour, while in more prosaic expressions the stimulus may be quite simply economic.

The transformation of corn poppy from weed of the hedgerows to garden plant owes much to the Reverend Wilks of Shirley. Although early in the sixteenth century writers were extolling the beauties of richly-coloured, full double poppies, it was not until the late-nineteenth century that the potential of the corn poppy was appreciated. While he was out walking, Reverend Wilks noticed a wild red poppy which had a white edge to the petals. In due course, he collected seed from this unusual variant and sowed it, no doubt, as most gardeners still do in similar circumstances. He then waited with some impatience for the seedlings to bloom. Selecting only those which showed a variation in flower to bear seed, he discarded all the rest. By selection and re-selection over several years he eventually established the famous Shirley poppy strain which has delighted succeeding generations of gardeners. Although the large, brilliantly coloured, soft-textured flowers last only a short time, new ones are produced in such numbers that blossoming extends over several months. A bed of Shirley poppies in full bloom on a bright August day, in all shades of rose, crimson, pink, and salmon is, indeed, a caprice of summer. The seed may be sown where the plants are to flower, then thinned after germination to 12 to 15 inches (30 to 38 cm) apart. Under normal soil conditions they grow approximately 24 inches (60 cm) high.

Oldest in cultivation, *P. somniferum*, the opium poppy, grows wild in Greece and the Orient. The very large red, purple, pink, or white flowers carried above grey, green leaves followed by the ornamental seed pods, make an imposing picture. The variety 'Pink Chiffon' has double pink flowers and

Below and right: *Papaver somniferum*

Above and right: Various colour forms of *Papaver nudicaule*, the Iceland poppy

is an attractive plant. That this species was originally grown for its edible seeds seems very probable, for I can find no mention of the plant's narcotic properties in early writings on the subject. The seeds do yield a nutty-flavoured, nutritious oil, and this was used instead of olive or almond oil for cooking. Nothing was wasted in the process, as the mash left after expression was fed to cattle or poultry. The seeds mixed with flour and honey were also made into cakes. Apart from being the source of opium which is the principal product of *P. somniferum*, the seed-heads were used to make a sedative in syrup form, and as a hot poultice for external application.

The drug opium is derived from the milky sap which exudes from incisions made in the half-ripe seed capsule. Opium possesses sedative powers, is a valuable medicine, and yields the pain-killing drug known as morphine. When abused, it destroys the health of mind and body.

As a garden plant the species is a beautiful, easily grown hardy annual, popular since the seventeenth century, though

not universally so, to judge from the name given to the flowers in Elizabethan times – Jack Silverpin, fair without, foul within. To some, the flowers do have an unpleasant smell. In present day seed catalogues there are many varieties on offer, though if Dutch flower paintings depicting the poppy are any guide, this is by no means a modern phenomenon.

The old variety *P. somniferum paeoniaeflorum* with double peony-like flowers is simplified in modern catalogues to peony-flowered, double mixed. Seed sown during April into well-drained sunny corners will in due season yield plants 2½ feet (75 cm) high bearing full double flowers in many and varied colours. To get the best effect the seedlings must be thinned to stand 12 to 15 inches (30 to 38 cm) apart. The old fashioned Latin form *mursellii* has been translated to the easily understood carnation-flowered, which accurately describes the attractively fringed, brightly coloured petals.

P. nudicaule, the Iceland poppy, is native to the arctic regions, and shows marked variations in flower even in the wild

species. Originally introduced during the eighteenth century, Iceland poppies are valuable for garden decoration and as early blooming plants to provide cut flowers. In my experience, they are best treated as biennials under cultivation. Seed is sown where the plants are to flower, then, when the seeds are large enough to handle, singled out at 12 inches (30 cm) apart for smaller growing varieties, or 18 inches (45 cm) apart for taller forms. They will flower the first summer from seed sown under glass in February. Though variations are listed under latinised names in specialist catalogues, the modern seed list offers a whole range of new colour forms. The Kelmscott strain provides a mixture of pastel shades including pink, golden-yellow and orange. The Iceland poppy has a light, elfin quality that contrasts pleasantly with the more statuesque perennials grown in gardens. When required for decoration indoors, the stems should be cut in the early morning just as the buds begin to open. The stalk end can be sealed by dipping the bottom inch or so in boiling water to make the flower stay fresh longer.

The alpine poppy, *P. alpinum*, is familiar to all those who enjoy mountains and the flowers which grow on them. It is a short-lived perennial which, if appearances are any guide, is very closely related to the arctic poppy, though smaller in height and reaching only up to 8 or 10 inches (20 or 25 cm). Seeds scattered along convenient open spaces in rock garden or border are all the introduction the species needs to be made to feel at home. Colour forms do exist, possibly produced from an alliance with *P. nudicaule*, and all are charming in an informal way. Another member of the family which can be grown as an alpine is *P. miyabeanum*. This has attractive yellow flowers and hails from Japan.

P. setigerum is very like the opium poppy in appearance, and is a native of the Mediterranean region. It has deeply cut leaves and violet flowers, and is an annual well worth having, being easy to grow from seed sown direct into the garden. I suspect that many of the cultivated varieties of opium poppy in catalogues, showing hairy divided leaves and purple shaded violet flowers, are the product of cross-pollination between the two closely related species.

Far left: *Papaver alpinum* in Switzerland
Left: *Papaver miyabeanum*

Below: *Papaver orientale* 'Goliath'

The two most interesting long-lived species for the garden both came from Armenia. Although less widely grown than *P. orientale*, the brightly coloured oriental poppy, *P. lateritium* with orange flowers carried on 18-inch (45-cm) stems in early summer is a species to note. For the small garden its neat compact growth and modest spread are worth considering as an advantage. The oriental poppy, *P. orientale*, has the gift of self-expression, for when carrying a full crop of flowers they are an eye-catching sight. They do need a lot of space to accommodate flower stems which sprawl most indolently, instead of soaring up to display the flowers which can be 10 inches (25 cm) or more in diameter. There is an air of triumphant, albeit garish opulence about the oriental poppy which is hard to ignore. Fortunately, there are cultivars which are

Above:
Papaver orientale 'Black and White'
Left: *Papaver orientale* 'Mrs Perry'
Below: *Meconopsis cambrica*

smaller than the 4 feet (1.2 m) high species which dominated the borders in Victorian gardens. Certainly, they are not particular as to soil, though like all the clan they luxuriate in a free-draining, light loam with a place in full sun. Propagation of new stock is simplicity itself. Young growth cut away with a section of root, or just sections of the fleshy root itself will rapidly establish and grow into vigorous young plants.

Of the well-established cultivars, 'Marcus Perry' is more upright growing than most others, with orange-scarlet flowers on 30-inch (75-cm) stems. Of the same clan, 'Mrs Perry' with salmon pink flowers is slightly dwarfer in stature. 'Goliath' frequently produces leaves on the stems, and I suspect it may be the result of a cross between *P. orientale* and *P. bracteatum*. Its flowers are crimson-scarlet, topping 3-feet (90-cm) high stems. Others which I admire are 'Black and White' with white flowers and a black centre, and low-growing 'Oriana' with ruffled orange flowers.

The layman's definition of poppy covers a broader spectrum than that of the botanist. A good example would be the genus *Meconopsis*, the name roughly translated means poppy-like, which is an apt description of the flower.

The Welsh poppy is our only native species, the rest grow in the Himalayan region, western China, Burma, and northern

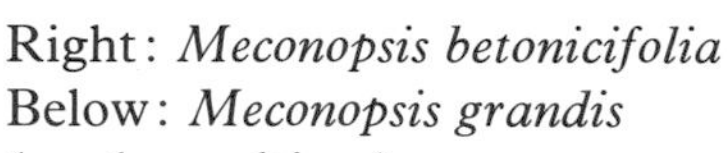

Right: *Meconopsis betonicifolia*
Below: *Meconopsis grandis*
(garden cultivar)

India. Though in the poppy family, few *Meconopsis* take kindly to hot dry conditions beloved of the Papaveraceae family. *Meconopsis cambrica*, the Welsh poppy is a perennial which, except in double-flowered forms, seeds so freely as to become a nuisance in the garden. The double variety *M. cambrica floreplena* with yellow or orange flowers, is rather like a miniature Shirley poppy (cultivars of *Papaver rhoeas*) and is a pleasant little perennial.

Best known of the species is the blue Himalayan poppy, *M. betonicifolia*, introduced from western China in 1924. The colour of the flowers, a vibrant sky blue in the best forms, with contrasting yellow stamens, made the plant immediately and deservedly popular. Seed, if sown fresh, germinates with commendable speed when put into lime-free, peat-based compost. Mature plants will also suffer division if this is done just as growth starts in spring. Prepare a bed in lime-free soil with plenty of humus, rotted farm manure, leaf-mould, or peat (all are equally suitable), preferably in a position with light shade from nearby but not overhanging trees. The flowering stems grow up to 4 feet (1.2 m) high.

M. grandis has flowers of vivid blue. The large four-petalled blooms, sometimes more in crown buds, are carried one to a stem in early summer. There are two exceptional forms

Left: *Meconopsis grandis* (Sikkim form)
Above: *Meconopsis integrifolia*

of this most outstanding perennial: one collected by George Sheriff and still sold under the collector's field number G.S.600, and the other called 'Slieve Donard' which came to me from the one-time nursery of that name in Northern Ireland. My plant, which carries a dozen or more very large sky-blue flowers open all at the same time, is a treasure beyond price.

M. quintuplinerva which rambles most happily in peaty soil, produces lavender-blue bells of flowers on 18-inch (45-cm) stems for several weeks during early summer. No plant I have grown sets seed, so recourse must be made to division of the parent, which is easy enough to accomplish in March or April. Reginald Farrer describes seeing the plant on the rolling alps of the Da Tung chain; so beautiful, he says, 'it made the senses ache.' *M. superba* in white makes a happy complement.

Though not a perennial, *M. napaulensis* is so lovely that sowing seed to ensure its continuity in the garden will seem a small price to pay. My plants grow for one or two seasons before sending up a 6- to 8-feet (1.8- to 2.4-m) flowering stem. The colour of petal varies from pink, red, blue, purple, or occasionally white on different plants. They are carried nodding on side branches all up the stem. Another Himalayan species that makes an attractive garden flower is *M. integrifolia*. It has long, pale green, hairy leaves and large yellow flowers.

To overcome the handicap of a name like *Eschscholtzia* and still become popular, a plant would need exceptional qualities. Better known as the Californian poppy, *E. californica* is a charming plant to grow. Beautiful and variable in flower with finely divided grey foliage as a complement, this is a lovely 12 to 24 inch (30 to 60 cm) high annual.

There are many named cultivars in seed catalogues. All thrive when sown into well-drained soil directly where they are to flower. The double-flowered 'Ballerina' and 'Harlequin' hybrids offer a good colour mixture. For the rock garden the 6 inch (15 cm) high yellow-petalled 'Miniature Primrose' is most attractive.

Meconopsis grandis 'Slieve Donard' in the author's garden

Above: *Glaucium flavium* in Greece
Right: *Argemone grandiflora* in California

Horned poppy and sea poppy are two popular names for *Glaucium*, natives of Europe and western Asia which are notable for their ornamental foliage and handsome flowers. I have cultivated only one species the horned poppy, *Glaucium flavium*, which grows wild in coastal areas of Britain. A short-lived perennial which reaches 1 to 2 feet (30 to 60 cm) high. The leaves are silver, flowers orange-yellow measuring 2 inches (5 cm) across. There are cultivars with spotted or particoloured petals, though these are not readily available. For me at least, the horned poppy leaves much to be desired as a garden plant.

Usually a plant's popularity can be measured by the number of nicknames it acquires. *Argemone*, another of the Papaveraceae family, has many and to spare: Mexican poppy, prickly bobby, devil's or infernal fig, yellow thistle or argemony – all of which argue that the plant should be better known. Only in hot dry summers do the Mexican poppies smother themselves with an abundance of large flowers. Seed can be sown under glass in March or outdoors in early May. I have grown *Argemone grandiflora* with white blossoms, and the yellow *A. grandiflora lutea*. Both reached 36 inches (90 cm) high and flowered abundantly in the hot, dry summers of 1975 and 1976. Results since then have been less encouraging. *A. mexicana* fared the same. Less upright in growth and when bedecked with bright yellow-orange flowers which give off a rather musky fragrance it excited considerable interest.

Once outside the limits prescribed by the botanists, the list grows beyond controllable numbers, so I will end with the tree poppy, *Romneya coulteri*, a Californian native species and a true perennial. The glaucous stems and deeply-cleft leaves support a succession of large white poppy-like flowers, enhanced with a golden centre of stamens. A warm sunlit place and well-drained soil is to this delightful shrub's taste. Propagation is by suckers, which are freely produced on established plants, or by means of root cuttings taken in November.

Romneya coulteri in southern California

10
Heathers

Heather is a collective name used to refer to three different genera of plants which to the layman look very much alike, yet to the botanist are quite separate. The best known in Great Britain, because it occupies such large tracts of land, is *Calluna vulgaris*, the ling or heather of the moors. Though *Calluna* may be the best known of the race, having only one species it is the smallest genus. The name *Calluna* is derived from a Greek word meaning clean – a reference to the use of ling stems for making brooms or besom. Ling grows wild over most of Europe from Norway to Spain, with a last outpost in North Africa.

There are five hundred and more species of *Erica*. No less than four hundred and seventy of these grow naturally in South Africa. Several more of the species inhabit tropical and North Africa, while Europe lays claim to those that remain. Five species are generally accepted as being indigenous to Britain and Ireland.

The third genus is of more manageable size. Saint Dabeoc's heath, Cantabrian heath, or Irish wort, the *Daboecia* of botanists is named after one of Ireland's many saints, St Dabeoc. Linnaeus mis-spelled the rather obscure saint's name by transposing the e and o, so *Dabeocia* became *Daboecia*. Two species and cultivars bred or derived from them are of garden usefulness; they are closely allied to, and need the same soil conditions as *Calluna* and *Erica*.

The ling, *Calluna vulgaris*, has not long been cultivated as a garden plant, only since early in the nineteenth century, if writers of the time are a true guide. Possibly this is explained by the firmly held conviction that ling would not grow when uprooted from the fells which it covers so luxuriantly in the wild.

For those people who farm close to the heather line, life has never been easy. The shallow, acid soil yields no more than a subsistence living, and great use had to be made of any materials lying ready to hand. Heather was pressed into service for roofing; the stems twisted into ropes secured thatch against gale force winds. Serviceable brooms could be fashioned from the stiff, hard stems of this tough little shrub. Indeed, one of the 'wet day' jobs in my early gardening days was making up

Above: *Erica regia* in glorious colour in South Africa

Left: *Calluna vulgaris*

besoms by lashing heather stems to handles made from coppiced hazel. A besom is still my first choice as a means of sweeping clean the lawn.

Highlanders and many north countrymen still consider that good fortune comes to those who find a patch of white heather. In even earlier times the Picts made beer from heather. Unfortunately, the secret manufacturing process was never divulged to strangers, and so was lost when this most mysterious race was dispersed. Fresh flowering shoots were used in the treatment of kidney infections, as an antiseptic, diuretic and cleansing mixture. In addition, heather contains tannin for curing leather and a yellow dye for colouring wool. Its use as a fuel to heat a bread oven, accorded it almost the same high rating as hawthorn. All things considered, heather was an important constituent of the upland economy. More significantly,

it is an important fodder crop for sheep, deer, and grouse, and is 'farmed' as such by the shepherds of the moors.

Old plants will, in time, grow tall and woody, producing few young shoots suitable for grazing. By burning off sections of the moor each year, the grazier farmers ensure a constant supply of young shoots and a complete rejuvenation of the heather crop. Indeed, tenant farmers in their leasehold since the fifteenth century have agreed to burn off a percentage of the heather on their 'stint' holding annually.

The botanical difference between *Calluna* and *Erica* is easily discovered by looking at the flower. In *Calluna*, the calyx is enlarged and coloured to become the ornamental part of the flower. The *Erica* is traditional in formation having the calyx green and the corolla as the coloured portion. Ling in the language of flowers is a symbol of solitude. Aptly so, for this small yet durable shrub shares its habitat with alpine flowers where human intrusion is the exception. Ling inhabits a terrain which is harsh in climatic terms and not over-rich in plant food. A typical moorland soil consists of acid peat which forms under conditions of high rainfall and a short growing season. Plant debris accumulates quicker than the soil organisms can break it down, and so the partially decomposed material builds up in layers of what we call peat.

In spite of growing under very specialised conditions of soil and climate, *Calluna* will adapt to a wide variety of soils in garden cultivation with one notable exception. I have never seen ling thriving in a lime soil, no matter how much effort and expensive mulching of peat or watering with trace elements was lavished on their cultivation. Given an acid or neutral soil, rich in humus, *C. vulgaris* in all the many forms available, ranging from low-creeping plants to shrubs a metre or more in height, will prove easy to grow. The most suitable soil is one which has

Calluna vulgaris 'Robert Chapman'

Calluna vulgaris 'Alba Rigida'

Calluna vulgaris 'Beoley Gold' at Bressingham Gardens, Norfolk

been well-prepared with dressings of peat or leaf mould, and is not liable to waterlogging in winter or excessive drying out in summer. *C. vulgaris* flowers in summer and autumn, but varieties are available with coloured foliage, which extends the interest over much of the year.

In an over-rich soil the plants put on vegetative growth at the expense of flowers, so, apart from an annual mulch of peat, any supplementary feeding must be done with care. Annual trimming of the old flower stems will prevent the plants growing leggy and untidy. Done correctly in spring, just before new growths break, they will make well-furnished compact shrubs. A typical ling shoot consists of fresh green-growing tip, then the flowers clustered round the stem, and below the flowers more green foliage. Clipping removes all this shoot including tip and dead flowers just into the green foliage below the old flower stems. Left unpruned, the green tip above the flowers grows ever upwards, while the stem below develops into a 'trunk' devoid of leaves or branches.

Planting is best carried out in the spring in most cases. Make a hole deep enough to accommodate the roots comfortably without constricting them in any way. The finished level should leave the junction between root and stems buried about one inch (2.5 cm) below the soil surface. A mulch of peat after planting will additionally encourage roots to develop from the buried stems, giving an altogether stronger feeding area.

The number of variations from the single species, many of them occurring naturally, is quite remarkable. Of the white flowered varieties, 'Beoley Elegance' with single blooms and 'Alba Rigida' carrying fully double blossoms are useful. 'Beoley Gold' and 'Robert Chapman' are coloured foliaged plants. Of those with double coloured flowers I would choose 'Elsie Purnell', 'H. E. Beale', 'Peter Sparkes', and 'Radnor'.

Though most of the European species of *Erica* were introduced in the last quarter of the eighteenth century, it was not until seeds of two tender South African species arrived in this country that an impetus was given to their popularity. By 1823 over four hundred erica species were in cultivation. The Empress Josephine, an enthusiastic horticulturalist, imported collections of erica from England, although France was at war with Great Britain during that period. These were used to form the basis of a famous heather garden in the grounds of Malmaison. Though beautiful, Cape heaths are not hardy, and it needs considerable skill and experience to grow them well. Nevertheless, royal patronage and the demand created by British gardeners encouraged exploitation of the potential value of the hardy European heaths as garden plants. This worked to such good effect that, although Cape heaths have a limited commercial success for sale as pot plants, the hardy European species enjoy immense popularity as colourful, informal, labour-saving plants.

The hardy species can be grouped under two headings. The tall or 'tree' heaths, which really are the 'giants' of the erica world, grow wild – mainly in Spain, Portugal, and around the Mediterranean. The remaining, and by far the larger group are low growing; five of the species being native to Britain. All of our native plants appear to be lime haters, at least this is my experience. Fortunately, *Erica herbacea* (syn. *E. carnea*), the mountain or Austrian heath from central and southern Europe, is not upset by lime and will grow well in quite alkaline soils. When it was brought to this country in 1763, gardeners grew the newcomer under glass, assuming it to be less than hardy. In fact, *E. herbacea*, the most important species in the genus, ranks amongst the toughest, most resilient shrubs ever to grace our gardens. Flowering as it does from October right through the icy months into early spring, its forms are amongst the most popular of winter flowering shrubs. It is of interest that most of the original work of raising and distributing new varieties was carried out by the nursery firm, Backhouse of York.

Above: *Erica herbacea* 'Myreton Ruby'

Left: *Erica massoni* growing in the South African mountains
Right: *Erica herbacea* 'Springwood White'

The cultivar 'Springwood White', found growing on Monte Corregio in Italy early this century, is a typical example of how so many of the most popular varieties have occurred naturally. One of the best, 'Springwood White' gained an Award of Merit in 1930, followed by an Award of Garden Merit in 1940 from the Royal Horticultural Society. Other excellent varieties selected from the many that are available are 'Eileen Porter', carmine rose – possibly not pure bred *E. herbacea*; 'March Seedling', pale purple; 'King George', deep rose-pink; 'Myreton Ruby', bright red; and 'Vivellii', deep carmine red. Forms having yellow, purple, or bronze foliage are also available, with 'Foxhollow' and 'Anne Sparkes' as possibly the most attractive.

E. cinerea, bell heather, a shrub of 6 to 18 inches (15 to 45 cm) high, enjoys a general distribution over the moors of Britain. Flowering just before the ling, the bright purple, egg-shaped flowers are carried in such profusion that they hide the dark green leaves. Though seemingly adapted to a wide range of soils, bell heather takes more managing in the garden than the redoubtable *E. herbacea*. Given a well-drained, lime-free soil, yet one which holds moisture in a dry summer, bell heather will thrive and put on a brave show throughout the summer to overlap with ling in the autumn.

Amongst the dozens of varieties on offer, some produce flowers in long terminal clusters, others blossom close to the foliage. The stronger-growing, long-stemmed types may be trimmed in much the same way as ling. I delay this pruning until the spring, for the russet-bronze dead blooms are pleasant enough to see on a hoar frosted winter's day. I have one qualification: the 'bells' open at intervals, so both the fresh and dead florets intermingle – not so pleasing as a hearty all-out display. There are numerous colour variations to choose from. Of those with white petals, 'Alba Major' and 'Alba Minor' are noteworthy. The rose-pink 'My Love', and 'Ann Berry' are deservedly popular, while 'Coccinea' is deep ruby red and very compact.

Coloured foliage forms are always interesting. 'Ann Berry', gold in winter, and 'Apricot Charm', light yellow with apricot tints are useful with all the year round leaf tints for the garden.

The cross-leaved heath, *E. tetralix* grows in the wetter moorland hollows, but under garden conditions any soil which does not dry out in summer (so long as it is lime-free) will prove acceptable to this most amiable heath. The flowers open from June to October in dense heads at the tips of the current season's growth. A trim over with shears, followed by a top dressing of moist peat rubbed well down amongst the stems will ensure the shrub's continued good health. The soft-textured foliage is silvery-grey rather than green, and thus makes an attractive feature. 'Alba Mollis', white, 'Hookstone', pink, and 'Con Underwood', crimson purple, are worthwhile additions to a collection.

Above: *Erica tetralix* 'Hookstone'

Left: A heather garden in summer with *Erica herbacea* providing the foliage interest
Right: *Erica cinerea* 'Ann Berry'

E. ciliaris, the Dorset heath, forms a shrub 6 to 15 inches (15 to 38 cm) high that is rather straggly and untidy in general appearance. As would be expected from the popular name, this beautiful native grows wild in the West Country, also in western Ireland and south western Europe. To some extent, the naturally sprawling habit of growth can be corrected by lightly clipping the plants over early in the spring. A lime-free soil and a regular top dressing of peat will suit this species. In my last two gardens, both in Yorkshire, *E. ciliaris* was killed off completely by winter frost one year in three, so it cannot be classified as completely hardy. Flowering from late summer into autumn, it is worth persevering with. Of the white-flowered cultivars, 'David McClintock' is good, but the flowers are pink-tinged at times. 'Corfe Castle' with clear salmon flowers is quite unusual, while 'Maweana', in gardens which offer a kinder climate than mine, with its grey foliage and dark pink blooms is quite lovely.

Left: a beautiful view of *Erica arborea* in northern Spain
Right: *Erica arborea alpina* in a garden setting

Above: *Erica lusitanica* 'George Hunt'
Below: *Erica lusitanica*

Of all the taller growing, or tree heaths, *E. arborea* pleases me the most. In favourable areas it will grow 20 feet (6 m) high, while still retaining a bushy shrub-like habit. The foliage is pale green, carried thickly up the stems. Its white flowers which appear early in March following a mild winter are very fragrant. One would expect a plant native to southern Europe, North Africa and Asia Minor to be so intolerant of conditions in this country as to be not worth growing. Yet in my last garden, two groups of *E. arborea* survived for twenty years, and only showed scorching of the foliage, which necessitated a clip-over with secateurs the following April. These plants were the variety *E.a. alpina* introduced to Kew Gardens at the turn of the century. As it was found growing in Spain on mountain slopes some 5000 feet (1500 m) above sea level, maybe it finds our climate almost congenial.

Erica arborea alpina 'Gold Tips' grew for seven years in my care, then succumbed to the winter of bitter memory 1981–82. Young growths in spring are yellow with just a hint of orange. A sheltered place is essential to the preservation of all *E. arborea*. As with all heathers, cuttings root so readily that any losses can be cheaply and easily made good.

E. lusitanica can grow up to a height of 10 feet (3 m) and spread up to 3 feet (0.9 m). A fairly hardy species, it has pink flower buds and a profusion of white flowers in the springtime. A particularly good garden form is 'George Hunt'. When crossed with *E. arborea*, an attractive shrub with white, scented flowers was produced – *E. × veitchii*. The only known garden form is 'Exeter'.

Erica × veitchii 'Exeter' in the Savill gardens

E. australis, the southern or Spanish tree heath, usually reconciles a tree-like inclination to a shrub reality by growing only 3 or 4 feet (0.9 to 1.2 m) high. A native of Spain and Portugal, it flowers during the spring and on occasions in early summer. Hard frosts kill top growth back to soil level, which is why mature plants are such a rare feature in gardens. The flowers are an attractive shade of red purple, although colours do vary from this to pale pink and white.

Heathers, like other familiar shrubs, have suffered name changes. *E. mediterranea* must now and henceforth, until botanists decree otherwise, be known as *E. erigena*. It is lime-tolerant, growing in cultivation up to 10 feet (3 m), but between 4 and 6 feet (1.2 and 1.8 m) is more usual in northern gardens. The wood of this species is extremely brittle, snow and strong winds breaking whole branches asunder. They do, however, refurbish themselves from soil level if the damaged stems are pruned away. It is native to Spain, south western France, and western Ireland, which is where most of the varieties grown in gardens originate. The rosy-red flowers with a fragrance of sun-warmed honey make a picture to rejoice the eye. The plants I saw on a lough side in Ireland, their flowers a haze of pink against a green and blue landscape, had that ethereal quality which no words can describe. The best-known variety is

Erica australis

Erica erigena 'Brightness'

'Brightness', 24 inches (60 cm) high, with dark foliage and pink flowers. 'W. T. Rackliff' has bright green foliage topped by a profusion of white flowers, and 'Superba' with two-toned flowers of rose-tinted purple. 'Superba' can grow up to 6 feet (1.8 m) high – a most impressive sight when in full bloom on a bright spring day. 'Alba' has delicate white flowers.

Although native to Spain, Corsica, and Italy, *E. terminalis* showed no sign of damage in the twenty years I grew it in a central Yorkshire garden some six hundred feet (180 m) above sea level, but it attained only one third of the 9 feet (2.7 m) recorded elsewhere. The rose-red flowers are developed in clusters at the shoot tips from mid-summer to autumn. It is a quietly pleasant heath which will thrive in acid or alkaline soil. A form with deeper coloured flowers is available.

Possibly my particular regard for the Cornish heath, *E. vagans* stems from the fact that my first heather garden was made on heart-breakingly heavy clay soil, and this species thrived and flourished better than any others I planted. Native to Cornwall, France, Spain, and locally in Ireland, this species grows in the wild up to 30 inches (75 cm) and has rather washed-out flowers of pale pinkish purple from mid-summer to October. Garden forms include much improved varieties, which are neatly compact in growth with brightly coloured flowers. The white 'Lyonesse', bright rose 'St Keverne', and darker cerise-red 'Mrs D. F. Maxwell' together with the attractive foliage of 'Valerie Proudley' are first class beginnings to a collection. Given regular dressings of peat, they will grow tolerably well in limy soil.

With the increasing interest in heathers as decorative plants, efforts to supply new varieties by cross-pollination between related species was inevitable. Some of the earliest hybrids, however, came from chance cross-pollination which occurred when two different *Erica* species were grown alongside each other in a nursery garden. *E.* × *darleyensis*, which appeared some hundred years ago in a Derbyshire nursery, is the product of natural cross-pollination between *E. herbacea* (syn. *E. carnea*) and *E. erigena*. Stronger growing than *E. herbacea* but with the same long flowering season combined with *E. erigena*'s free blossoming character, the chance seedlings are a valuable addition to the range. Starting to flower in December and continuing until May, they span the bleakest months of the year:

'Arthur Johnson' with mauve pink flowers in long spikes,
'Darley Dale' the original hybrid with lilac rose blossom,
'George Rendall' lilac pink, and the white flowered
'Molten Silver' ('Silverschmelze') are good value.
'J. W. Porter' has attractive mauve-pink flowers.

Daboecia contains only two species and is quite different in appearance to the other heathers. As with *Calluna* and most *Erica* species, a lime-free soil is essential for their well-being. The individual egg-shaped flowers are large by comparison with those of the other heathers, appearing from late summer to early autumn. Once the flower 'sets' (is fertilised), the corolla drops and the dead stems can be trimmed away – a summary pruning which keeps the bush compact.

Daboecia azorica from the Azores was introduced in 1929, so it is still very much a newcomer. The deep red flowers hang pendant on stalks from the 4- to 6-inch (10- to 15-cm) high stems. The average height varies, depending on variety, between 10 and 12 inches (25 and 30 cm). *D. cantabrica* is, I think, of better constitution, certainly hardier than *D. azorica*, and taller growing – up to 18 inches (45 cm) or even more. The rosy purple flowers which are displayed from June to late October are carried on long, leafless stems, well clear of the dark green leaves. *D. cantabrica* is a native of Ireland and western Europe. A light loam with a generous admixture of peat, plus a clip over in spring to remove the spent flower stems and the tips of the previous seasons growth, is all the attention this attractive dwarf shrub requires. Cultivars of the recently introduced hybrid, *D.* × *scotica*, combine hardiness with compact growth.

Of all the varieties *D. cantabrica alba* is my favourite. The vivid green leaves supply a proper contrast to the large, pure white floral bells. 'Hookstone Purple' with purple flowers, and 'Praegerae' with salmon-pink bells are very fine dwarf shrubs, and the latter exceptionally so.

Left: *Erica vagans* 'Valerie Proudley'
Right: *Daboecia cantabrica* 'Praegerae'

Propagation of *Calluna*, *Erica*, and *Daboecia* is easily achieved either by means of cuttings or layering. Non-flowering shoots of the current season's growth taken in the season June to October are suitable. Equal parts of fine-grade sphagnum moss, peat and sharp lime-free sand or crushed granite make a good cutting compost. Unless large quantities of cuttings are required, dibble the cuttings into a 6-inch (15-cm) pot of the above compost, then plunge the container into a frame. Water only with lime-free water as required, and rooting should take place in 6 weeks or a little longer according to the season. Those taken in October may not be well-enough rooted for potting off until the following spring.

Layering is the fool-proof method. Selected plants growing in the garden need only be mounded up with the peat-sand mixture, so that the base of the stems are covered. Sufficient roots have usually formed after 6 to 8 months for the layer to be removed. Better results are gained by pegging down selected branches into compost with pegs made from heavy duty galvanised wire.

A heather border makes a pleasant, labour-saving feature. By careful choice from the varieties on offer of *Daboecia*, *Erica*, and *Calluna* it is possible to have plants to bloom for all the twelve months in the year. Maintenance is minimal, for apart from clipping and mulching, the weeding is reduced by the living ground cover of heather foliate.

Left: *Erica × darleyensis* 'J. W. Porter'

Index

References to illustrations are printed in bold-face type.